Universe as Revelation

Jo Farrow's earliest experience of the holy was her awareness of the earth as sacred space. That awareness has persisted and deepened and continues to be her most vivid experience of the holy. She joined the Society of Friends in 1995 and is a member of Littlehampton meeting. She records her experience in her autobiography, *The World in My Heart: A personal exploration of spirituality and awareness,* published in 1990 by Quaker Home Service. She received a grant from the Joseph Rowntree Charitable Trust to write this book.

Alex Wildwood has been influenced by a variety of spiritual paths and traditions. Brought up in a culturally Christian context, he became a Marxist and atheist at college. In his late twenties he discovered the Goddess and began celebrating pagan festivals. He now most readily encounters the Mystery in elemental nature, open-hearted sharing with other people and in accepting his own brokenness; he has been called a 'neo-Buddhist' and told he has 'a ministry of vulnerability'. A member of the Religious Society of Friends since 1988, he works as a freelance speaker, writer, facilitator and retreat leader. He gave the 1999 Swarthmore Lecture, published as *A Faith to Call Our Own* (Quaker Home Service) and co-authored, with Timothy Ashworth, *Rooted in Christianity, Open to New Light: Quaker spiritual diversity* (Pronoun Press/Woodbrooke) in 2009.

Universe as Revelation:

An ecomystical theology for Friends

Jo Farrow &
Alex Wildwood

Published 2013 by Pronoun Press

Pronoun Press is an imprint of Peter Daniels Publisher Services
35 Benthal Road, London N16 7AR, UK
www.pronounpress.co.uk

ISBN 978-0-9556183-7-6

Published with the support of the Joseph Rowntree Charitable
Trust, York.

List of Contents

Preface

There is science now to construct the story of the journey we have made on this Earth, the story that connects us with all beings ... Right now on our planet we need to remember that story – to harvest it and taste it. For we are in a hard time, a fearful time. And it is the knowledge of the bigger story that is going to carry us through ... Let us remember it together.

Joanna Macy[1]

This book has evolved considerably over time. It began when Jo Farrow retired from working at Friends House and was encouraged to write something that made accessible to other denominations the distinctive flavour of contemporary Quaker life. Surprisingly, while there was a wealth of writing about Quaker history and Quaker enterprises, no one had written about how these weave together with the Quaker experience behind them, and how they create a way of living, a kind of ethical mysticism that might be called our Quaker spirituality.[2]

A number of factors combined to alter the nature of the book. Soon after starting the project, Jo became ill. Having spent the greater part of her working life ignoring the quite legitimate claims of the body in favour of the mind and spirit, now, in retirement, her body protested about that long neglect. Reflecting on the alchemy of illness gave her a greater sense of urgency to write about the hierarchy of values which places 'Spirit' above 'Body', and self-denial above pleasure and enjoyment of the natural world. Trained in classical Christian theology, Jo was only too aware of the many devotional books, some of them classics, which elevate mind and spirit above body, and how for some of

---

[1] *Thinking Like a Mountain*, pp. 57–60.

[2] In the States, Douglas Steere wrote a brief introduction to the anthology *Quaker Spirituality* 1983/1995. John Lampen edited a small volume *Wait in the Light: The Spirituality of George Fox*, 1981.

their authors the body is even despised and rejected. In contrast, the New Creation Story – which now lies at the heart of this book – is the story of the physical universe as revealed to us by science; it is at its core a story of embodiment and offers a life-affirming, sacred story for our time.

Early in retirement, Jo led a series of workshops on Quaker spirituality in New Zealand, where she shared with other Quaker women the nature of their spiritual experiences. This strengthened her conviction that all religious traditions have tended to assume that male perceptions about faith and practice tell the whole story. But on her return to England Jo's health deteriorated further – to the point where she had little energy and writing for any length of time became a real difficulty. By now she had several chapters written but didn't have the strength to complete a book. Knowing that what she was writing about resonated with several themes in my 1999 Swarthmore lecture, she suggested a collaboration on what then became an essentially different book.

Jo had been looking at a number of what she called 'doom and gloom' studies of contemporary Quaker life in Britain. These were serious studies and while she did not necessarily dissent from their findings, she found herself drawing quite different conclusions to their authors. She could not agree with their common view that twenty-first century Friends were somehow vastly inferior to the seventeenth century kind. And she was deeply suspicious of an insidious Quaker fundamentalism that would have us all fall into line and try to be clones of George Fox or Elizabeth Fry.

When a first draft of the book had just been completed the collaboration was interrupted while Alex worked with Timothy Peat Ashworth (tutor in Biblical Studies at Woodbrooke) offering an experiential process to meetings around the country which became the 'Rooted in Christianity; Open to New Light' project, and the book of the same title. This opportunity of 'travelling in the ministry' gave him the chance to begin developing many of the ideas that he writes about here. Both Alex and Jo, visiting meetings throughout Britain (and to a lesser extent in the wider Quaker world), have been amazed at the courage, risk-taking, and imagination of contemporary Friends. In virtually every meeting they found a core of Friends who were continuing the tradition of being both mystics and menders of the world. Yet in spite of affirmations about being non-credal, and our understanding that how we walk with God matters far more than how we talk about God, many Friends still seem to be worried that our failure to be articulate about the content of our faith, or about the immense, unfathomable, mystery of God, is a sign of some deficiency that will, in the not too distant future, bring about our demise as a religious society.

One final factor helped give the book its present form. Travelling with Tim, Alex encountered many Friends who wanted to see themselves as part of the long, frequently hidden, tradition of Creation-Centred Spirituality.[3] The task he and Jo finally set themselves as authors was to rediscover something of Friends' long-lost testimony to the goodness of Creation while setting this in the context of other, contemporary, movements of the Spirit that were informed by awareness of the ecological crises of our age. Matthew Fox, in his best-known book *Original Blessing* had named George Fox as one who belonged to the creation-centred tradition; and a study guide from Friends United Press suggests that a 'Testimony to the Goodness of Creation' was one of the earliest Quaker Testimonies.[4]

* * *

Friends in Britain have spent a lot of energy in recent decades worrying about our identity as a religious society and the correct ordering of ourselves and our structures. During this time there have been Friends who cautioned against excessive introspection and reminded us to turn our attention outwards, to focus on our witness in the world. In more recent years there has also been a clear acknowledgement of a spiritual hunger within the Yearly Meeting, a recognition of a need for spiritual renewal. It is our belief that the inspiration we are seeking, and the energy-

[3] See Matthew Fox, *Creation Spirituality: Liberating gifts for the peoples of the Earth.*

[4] Ben Richmond, *Testimonies*, pp. 22–25.

source we need to tap into in order to address the complex and demanding crises of our age, can be found in this exciting new awareness of who we are and the awesome universe we inhabit.

Inevitably this book reflects our differences as well as our shared enthusiasm for this 'new cosmology'. Jo's background and training are in traditional Christian theology, albeit with a critical feminist eye for its shortcomings and limitations; Alex's faith has been shaped by a wider variety of spiritual influences, especially Buddhist teachings on interdependence, and his experience of 'holistic' or contemporary spirituality. Early on we decided not to attempt a single, common voice (except in this Preface and the Introduction) but to let our different perspectives and experiences sit alongside one another.

We also felt that as much of what we are exploring would be new to many readers certain themes would bear a degree of repetition. We have chosen to interweave personal experience and reflection with the intellectual and conceptual. We hope that in this way the book will speak to readers on several different levels.

* * *

The book is offered as an invitation to explore an ecomystical theology – one that challenges some of Friends' theological assumptions of the last three hundred and sixty years while building on the many strengths of our tradition.

Given the long gestation of this book, our own views and understanding have necessarily grown and changed, calling for a series of revisions. With each reworking of the text new insights and further resources kept emerging; we reached a point where we realised we could go on revising indefinitely. We had to accept that we had a 'good enough' text for the purpose of opening up issues we felt were important for the yearly meeting to consider. The collective resolve of Britain Yearly Meeting in the summer of 2011 gave us the final incentive we needed to publish what we had written.

We are grateful to the many people who have played a part in the making of this book. First of all our gratitude goes to the

Trustees of the Joseph Rowntree Charitable Trust who saw fit to commission Jo to write the original book and who subsequently supported its change of direction by releasing Alex for a period of writing. Our thanks also go to the many participants on workshops and attentive listeners at our talks who have helped us develop out ideas and explore them in a Quaker context. We are grateful as well to those who read different drafts and chapters of what has been an evolving enterprise. Our thanks specially to Ben Pink Dandelion and Peter Daniels for helping give the book its present shape, to Seren Wildwood for editorial suggestions on an early draft, to Pam Lunn for some critical feedback, and to Jocelyn Burnell for checking some of the science.

Finally our heart-felt thanks to our partners, Seren Wildwood and Joan Miller, for putting up with so much and for supporting the demands of this writing in particular.

Jo Farrow and Alex Wildwood

Introduction

As we write this, a sense of radical change hangs in the air. In the mass media frequent references are made to the 'Arab Spring', the popular uprisings which have challenged tyrannical regimes in that part of the world recently. The crisis in the economies of the West has spawned the 'Occupy' encampments in financial centres around the world, forms of protest whose slogan 'We Are The 99% that will no longer tolerate the greed and corruption of the 1%' resonates with many of us.[1] And all such forms of social resistance are taking place against a backdrop of mounting evidence of global environmental degradation and growing ecological awareness and activism.

The consensus of scientific opinion now recognises that rises in the average temperature of the Earth's atmosphere and oceans are the result of human activity. There is also broad agreement that these temperature rises are likely to continue in a way that threatens life on Earth – and are already having a devastating impact on some of the most vulnerable human populations in the world. Daily the evidence mounts that we cannot continue with 'business as usual'; a sense of crisis and possibility permeates our waking consciousness and seeps into our dreams. We are living in what Dominican priest Albert Nolan characterises as 'an age full of promise but fraught with unimaginable dangers'.[2] Faced with imminent threats to our survival, growing numbers of people around the world are committing themselves to making peace with the planet, to creating a just and sustainable future for all.[3] The Transition initiative, a broad movement of 'community-led responses to climate change, inequality and shrinking supplies of cheap energy', began in the United Kingdom and has galvanised people around the world.[4]

This is the context in which Quakers in Britain, at Yearly Meeting Gathering at Canterbury in the summer of 2011, made

[1] For details of the 'Occupy' movement see occupywallst.org
[2] *Jesus Today* p. 45. [3] See Paul Hawken, *Blessed Unrest*.
[4] Now over a thousand communities around the world; see www.transitionnetwork.org and *The Transition Companion*.

'a strong corporate commitment to become a low-carbon, sustainable community'.[5] The minute recognised that the commitment we have collectively made will challenge us both as individuals and as meetings. We are invited to 'look again at our lifestyles and reassess our priorities', realising that within this corporate call to action, each individual and meeting may feel led to a different kind of faithful response. But Minute 36 also recognises that our concern 'grows from our faith and cannot be separated from it'.

As a religious community our responses to the threats we face (whether pragmatic, political, or prayerful, or all three) will necessarily arise from, and be informed by, how we understand and live out our Quaker faith. But today a great diversity of beliefs and spiritualities are gathered under the Quaker banner. This diversity is part of what gives us hope for the future as authors of this book. But we are also aware that we are living in a time of transition as a faith community, a time when some want to hang on to the familiar whilst others are ready to jettison the past. If our spiritual diversity is all too apparent, what is the source of our unity as British Friends today? Some would argue that it is our distinctive Quaker way of doing things; others that it is our testimonies. This book is founded on the belief that unity also needs to arise from telling a new story about ourselves, finding new ways of imagining and relating to the Source of our existence – creating a new theology, drawing on the work of visionary theologians, scientists, poets and evolutionary activists.

Faced with the urgent need to examine how we live and to take action to end the destructive habits of industrialised humanity that threaten the integrity of life on Earth, theology might seem something of a luxury. But theology in the sense of the religious story we tell ourselves about our origins, about the purpose and meaning of our lives, about how we each belong to 'a life larger and more lasting than our own'[6] – a story that can inspire us, that evokes in us a sense of awe and wonder and meets the human need for ecstasy and transcendence – is, we argue, exactly what is needed as we face the challenges ahead. A

---

[5] Britain Yearly Meeting 2011 Minute 36, also published as *Our Canterbury Commitment.*

[6] Gary Kowalski, *Science and the search for God*, p. 23.

new way of embracing the Mystery at the heart of life, founded on new understandings of who we are and the nature of the universe we inhabit, is essential to the transition humanity needs to make. And it is something which, we argue, Friends need to incorporate into our religious awareness. What faith communities need to bring to the tide of activism rising all around us is a new (yet often also ancient) awareness of the sacred mystery of existence: 'An absence of a sense of the sacred is the basic flaw in many of our efforts at ecologically or environmentally adjusting our human presence to the natural world.'[7]

Social and ecological activist Joanna Macy speaks of three kinds of action needed in this time. The first is hands-on activism, taking physical action in defence of species and habitats. The second is new ways of thinking about our situation, analysing how we got in this mess and imagining and realising alternative futures; this is the work mainly of our minds. And the third kind of activity is shifting human consciousness, imaging ourselves and our relationship to the rest of life in a new way – this is the work of our hearts. Theology of the kind we explore in these pages is heartwork.

This book invites the reader to explore a paradigm shift in awareness of who human beings are – a new framework within which we can make sense of everything we observe and experience. This reflects new understandings of the origins, evolution, and fundamental nature of the universe – all made possible by technological developments such as electron microscopes, space probes, and the Hubble Space telescope. One of the things that is exciting about this time is how many developments in science actually encourage rather than inhibit mystical awareness. Today we can appreciate that science, by so magnificently extending our human senses, actually enlarges our human capacity for awe and wonder.

There are many ways to characterise the spirit of our times but two identifying factors are particularly relevant here. First is the marked sense in the West today of a hunger for spirituality – which is directly related to a growing disillusionment with institutional forms of religion. At the same time, in spite of the constant

7 Thomas Berry's Foreword to *When the Trees Say Nothing*, p. 18.

assault of a ubiquitous advertising industry, more and more people are realising that a purely consumerist lifestyle or identity cannot bring fulfilment and is bought at the price of terrible global injustice and inequality. These two characteristics combine in a growing dissatisfaction with a crude materialism that makes no allowance for mystery. People today are hungry for spiritual experience, they want a religious story that makes sense to them, that does not fly in the face of reason or contradict our scientific understanding of reality. And there is one emerging today.

Ours is the first generation to have verified by observation that the universe itself has evolved, that is not a static 'thing' but a dynamic, continuously evolving process. The universe is not simply a place we live but an ongoing transformational event of which we are inherently a part. We know now that we are all made of the same basic stuff, the same elements of existence. We know that human beings are just one among millions of species; that we exist within a matrix of life that stretches back to single-celled creatures that first appeared 3.8 billion years ago, even beyond that to the birth of our solar system, and a further ten billion years to the first millisecond of the explosive origins of our universe. We are distant relations of that primal fireball and closer relatives of the stars. We carry traces of those profound beginnings in our blood and bones. This new cosmology has far-reaching implications, especially in the way it invites us to regain a sense of our connectedness, our interdependence with, the rest of life on Earth.

This 'Great Story', as Catholic cultural historian Thomas Berry calls it, this wondrous account of the emergence of our universe – revealed to us by science but understood as a sacred narrative – is our story. But it is also the story of everything that is. It is only in the last few decades that we have confirmed scientifically what mystics, children, poets, and artists have always known intuitively: that we are related to everything, that we are all participating in one vast, wondrous, energy-event we call 'the universe'. This is the source of our lives and it is to this that we all belong.

We can now appreciate that the universe-event, and our planet Earth with all its incredible diversity and complexity, emerged from a single pinpoint of energy, what scientists refer to as the original singularity. Hard as it is to grasp, everything that exists shares a common origin: from the furthest galaxies to the simplest forms of life, everything has a common history and is, in a distant or intimate way, related to everything else. Realising our common origin, witnessing the complexity and diversity which we see all around us, we can appreciate that diversity and unity are built into the very nature of the universe.

Embracing this science-based understanding of our genesis enables us to see the universe process itself as revelatory. In his seminal work, *The Dream of the Earth*, Thomas Berry suggests that the universe, the solar system and the Earth, rather than our written scriptures (which are always limited by cultural and historic specifics) need to be seen as 'the primary revelation of that ultimate mystery whence all things emerge into being'.[8] And the more scientists investigate both the furthest reaches of the galaxies and the strange nature and behaviour of matter at the subatomic level, the more mysterious the universe-process appears.

But the new cosmology also discloses to us something about the way we should live and how we can best understand our human destiny. The universe, according to mathematical physicist Brian Swimme, is a vast communion event, one which displays order and meaning – and a purpose which must include us. In his audiovisual presentation *Canticle to the Cosmos*, he describes the fundamental order of the universe, observing three basic laws or dynamics of the universe, which he names as differentiation, subjectivity and communion. Differentiation means, essentially, that every being is born with a quantum of energy and the task, laid upon us by the universe, is to become who we are. Subjectivity – or depth of being – means that everything has an interior as well as an exterior dimension. And communion simply means that 'to be is to be involved in the primordial web that links everything in the universe'.[9]

The ethics of the cosmos, in the light of this new understanding, are really quite simple. Whatever supports these three aspects of the universe is good. Whatever hinders them is not. Sadly, Swimme observes, our religious institutions have generally hindered rather than helped their adherents to become differ-

8 *The Dream of the Earth*, p. 107.   9 *Canticle to the Cosmos*, Session 4.

entiated, fully and completely themselves. This is tragic because what the Great Story encourages us to realise is that never before in the long history of our planet has there been another creature quite like any of us – and never in the future can there be another person with our particular gifts of creativity, our unique distinctive way of being.

This new revelatory experience, our present understanding of the nature of reality, points to an inherent intimacy between ourselves and the Earth – and invites us to rethink, for example, the Biblical drama of our beginnings. We now know that human beings were not created perfect and then spoiled the whole story by falling into sin. We also know that it has taken some ten billion years or so to prepare the way for the human experiment. In a continuously evolving universe there is certainly no shame in recognising that we are still very unfinished creatures. The 'Jesus event' – traditionally interpreted by the mainstream churches as being about atonement and a divine rescue mission – is perhaps more helpfully seen as being about the kind of evolutionary leap necessary if we are to survive as a species and find our true relationship to the rest of creation. Jesus may be the prototype of the new humanity, the one who gives us a clue about how a fully human being lives.

Similarly, we need to leave behind the Biblical notion of ourselves as beings created to have dominion over the Earth and its creatures – beings only a little lower than the angels, humanity as the crown of creation. The picture that is unfolding is much more humbling as well as more amazing. We are an intimate part of creation rather than above or separate from the rest. We are not so much the dramatic peak of the evolutionary enterprise as the recipients of gifts that have come to us from stars and plants, water, and bacteria, and every form of life we have thought of as lower or lesser than us. Without all the 'experiments' in non-human life and aspects of existence we have regarded as inanimate we should not be here at all. But we are also beings who have consciousness: we can know and celebrate the amazing story of the universe. We are the universe becoming conscious of itself. The new cosmology invites us to see our human destiny as being the enablers, the facilitators to the next phase in the ongoing story of the cosmos. And we can find clues as to how we might conduct ourselves – what a sustainable role for humanity might be – from our understanding of the universe itself.

Every second the sun transforms four million tons of itself into light. This vast outpouring of energy is photosynthesised by plants that are consumed by animals. This means that throughout our evolutionary journey humans have been feasting on the sun's energy stored in grain and vegetables and other animals. In this example of the sun we have a new understanding of the cosmological meaning of sacrifice: every minute of the day the sun is giving itself away to become the energy we need to live; in theological terms, this kenotic principle is built into the structure of the universe. Christians have long claimed that God in Jesus empties himself, gives himself away; now we can see that this kenosis or self-emptying of God is also a habit of the universe. We are here because of an amazing sequence of irreversible events during nearly fifteen billion years of the universe story – the Christian myth echoes the fact that life, sacrifice, death and resurrection are all woven into the story of the universe itself.

Don Cupitt makes this point in his essay on 'solar ethics'. The sun, he observes, 'is always in the process of living and dying. The nuclear burning by which it lives is also identically the process by which it is dying. Its whole being is wholly both at once ... It gives all that it has. You cannot ask for more than that.'[10]

In the end the ethics of the old and new theologies may not be so different. Cupitt's advocacy of solar ethics may well be the same point that Jesus is reported to have made, that those who give themselves away without concern for self-interest have discovered what life is all about, and those who hoard themselves like misers, giving nothing away, will, in the end find that their real life has been eroded.

The central question of any creation story and any cosmological exploration is 'Who are we?' When early Friends affirmed themselves as 'Children of the Light' they were using imagery borrowed from John's Gospel and Epistles. With our present understanding we might imaginatively suggest that they were making an intuitive affirmation of their cosmic lineage as 'children of the stars', distant descendants of those photons that reached back to the primal fireball and the birth of the first gal-

10 *Solar Ethics*, p. 14.

axies. In their use of imagery of light they were closer to the truth than they knew, closer than the New Testament writers realised. We are children of an experiment with Light that began nearly fifteen billion years ago and is still continuing.

Light is the vital component in all atoms and molecules. 'For every particle of matter there are 1 billion particles of light. The human body stores immense amounts of light.'[11] This is not what George Fox meant when he talked about the Inward Light, but it is the kind of awareness that today can take us beyond our ego-centric sense of self, outwards towards an identity rooted in the rest of existence.

The suffering of our world cries out for such an evolution of the human self. Sister of Mercy Nellie McLaughlin sees in the new story of the universe, 'a new transforming context for our lives, our hopes and dreams'. Its vision of 'the oneness of all life, one living system, one enchanting story for all', is emerging in this time out of 'the radical engagement between human spirituality and science. Herein the physical and spiritual development of the evolving Universe is synthesised for the first time.'[12]

It is our belief that Friends alive today – who are heirs to a consciousness informed by Darwinian evolution, quantum physics, and that image of the Earth from space – can find succour and inspiration, can discover a religious sensibility born of our times in the new story of the universe. It is our experience that this story can be a source of encouragement, a vital way of gaining perspective on our personal and communal lives as we face the challenging adventure of radical change together.

As Quakers we need to discern in our meetings those aspects of our tradition that are truly liberating; we need to re-discover those aspects of our spirituality that reflect a passionate concern for peace and justice – not only for the human species, but also for all inhabitants on this planet that we have plundered so aggressively. And we need to weed out those aspects of our religious tradition which are suspicious of life or do not support us to live a fully human life. Perhaps it is also time to be more focused on our potential to offer inclusive hospitality to spiritual travellers than to be brandishing and burnishing 'our Quaker

---

[11] Cited by Matthew Fox, drawing on various sources by scientific authors, in *Sins of the Spirit, Blessings of the Flesh*, p. 48.
[12] *Out of Wonder*, p. 203.

distinctives.' It is in the spirit of such a re-examination of our inheritance that we offer this book.

What we offer here is a series of reflections designed to get us all thinking about a contemporary theology that can energise us in our commitment to becoming a sustainable, low-carbon community. For as Pam Lunn says in the 2011 Swarthmore Lecture, 'we should not underestimate the place of theology in creating frameworks of meaning and purpose that can inspire and move us to action'.[13] If what we have written here can contribute in any way to a rekindling of Quaker faith in the context of the threats we face, to a spiritual understanding of how human beings can become a more sustainable presence on the Earth, this present volume will have served its purpose.

* * *

The book is divided into ten chapters, each one bearing the author's name. 'On the Edge of the New' considers how many of us today feel ourselves to be what John Shelby Spong calls 'believers in exile', unable to identify with doctrinal religion or the traditional biblical worldview. 'Living Between Stories' sets the new universe story in the context of the 'spirituality revolution' in the West, and suggests part of the contemporary search for spirituality is a response to the ecological crises we face, our sense of estrangement from the rest of life on Earth. 'Speaking to Our Condition' spells out the current destruction of the life-support mechanisms of our planet, introduces the concepts of 'The Great Turning' and 'deep time' and sets these in the context of the 'listening spirituality' of Friends and our coming of age as a species. 'Coming Down to Earth' looks at what it would mean to reclaim an Earth-centred spirituality, a theme taken up in 'Living Earth Spirit' which explores Gaia theory and the potential of Quaker worship for opening us to the mysterious wellsprings of Life present in the world around us. 'That's the Spirit' is a reflection on what we mean by Spirit in these exciting, evolutionary times – suggesting that we might usefully see it as the energy of life itself, whilst 'Universe as Revelation' invites us

13 *Costing Not Less than Everything*, p. 18

to move from 'believing in God' to acknowledging our kinship with the whole of reality. 'A God Who Stands Back' looks at how we live with the 'darkness' of God, how we deal with that aspect of the divine Mystery we experience as the absence of God. 'Faith in Transition' explores what post-doctrinal faith looks and feels like – taking 'faith' as a profound trust in life itself, as a radical sense of belonging, of knowing we really are part of the cosmic story we outline here. The final chapter, 'Glimpses of a New Spirituality' calls on us to realise our connection to the whole of life as a religious epiphany.

* * *

This emerging Universe Story and its theological implications may be new and unfamiliar, but there is plenty of scope for further study from sources we refer to. In the telling of this new story certain names inevitably recur – so we introduce them here for the convenience of our readers: Thomas Berry, Brian Swimme, Matthew Fox, and Miriam MacGillis have all been concerned to recover the lost creation-centred tradition of Christianity and to relate this to the story of the universe being revealed by modern science.

Thomas Berry (who died in 2009) was a Catholic cultural historian deeply influenced by the evolutionary philosophy of Teilhard de Chardin. Berry called himself a 'geologian' – a theologian of the Earth. In the last twenty years of his life he extended his Passionist Order's message of compassion and hope to include not just humanity but the whole of life on Earth, and his study of cultural history to embrace the evolution of the universe. He saw humanity as being in trouble right now because we are between stories: 'The old story, the account of how the world came to be and how we fit into it, is no longer effective. Yet we have not learned the new story.'[14]

Brian Swimme, a mathematical physicist, is Director of the Center for the Story of the Universe[15] and a profes-

14 *The Dream of the Earth*, p. 123; and thomasberry.org
15 www.storyoftheuniverse.org

sor at the California Institute of Integral Studies where he teaches evolutionary cosmology. He collaborated with Thomas Berry for over ten years and together they wrote The Universe Story: a celebration of the unfolding of the Cosmos. Swimme has also written *The Hidden Heart of the Cosmos* (Orbis, 1996) and produced three DVD series: *Canticle to the Cosmos*, *The Earth's Imagination*, and *The Powers of the Universe*. His most recent collaboration, with Mary Evelyn Tucker, has resulted in a book and DVD, *Journey of the Universe*.

Matthew Fox[16] is a theologian and activist, concerned with the renewal of education and religion. Originally a Dominican, he was silenced by the Catholic church and then accepted into the Episcopalians. He describes himself as 'a post-denominational priest' and is best known for his book *Original Blessing* and as a pioneering exponent of 'creation-centred spirituality'. His scholarly work has contributed much to the rediscovery of Hildegard of Bingen, Meister Eckhart, and Thomas Aquinas as pre-modern mystics and prophets.

Miriam Therese MacGillis[17] is the director and one of the co-founders of Genesis Farm – a community-supported agricultural project and residential centre in New Hampshire sponsored by the Dominican Sisters. A student of Thomas Berry's, she has been a passionate advocate of the Great Story for many years. In this capacity she gave one of the Schumacher lectures in 2004 and has spoken on 'the new cosmology' as part of the 'Alternatives' programme at St James's Church, Piccadilly, London. Her work is rooted in the belief that the universe, the Earth, and all reality 'are permeated by the presence and power of that ultimate Holy Mystery that has been so deeply and richly expressed in the world's spiritual traditions'. She currently teaches courses on 'the new cosmology', 'community resilience' and 'deep transition'.

[16] www.matthewfox.org
[17] www.genesisfarm.org

Chapter 1
On the Edge of the New

Jo Farrow

The Christian faith today has to be understood and practised within a new cosmic framework. The small stage offered by the Bible, which once was comforting, is no longer adequate ... We live in a new world with a wealth of scientific knowledge. By quiet attentiveness and contemplation we make ourselves prone to inspiration. As we integrate the symbols of faith into our own lives we will each of us find our own myth, our own inner story, which will hold all things together in a coherent vision.

Adam Ford[1]

The world today is on the verge of a new age and a new culture.

Bede Griffiths[2]

There have been moments in my life, as I believe there are in most lives, when something happens that marks the end of one way of life and the possibility of something new, but as yet unknown. In the Greek vocabulary of the New Testament there are two words for 'time'. One is 'chronos' – ordinary clock time, time measured from minute-to-minute, hour-to-hour. The other is 'chairos' – significant, 'out-of-the-ordinary' time – the time of grace and revelation.

It was a time like the latter for me in 1963 when I finished reading John Robinson's runaway best seller, *Honest to God*. In it he introduced people to Dietrich Bonhoeffer's 'religionless Christianity', and the 'death of theism', and Paul Tillich's model

[1] *Universe: God, Man and Science*, pp. 42 & 193.
[2] *A New Vision of Reality*, p. 9.

of God as 'the ground of our being'. I think that I must be a very slow learner. It has taken me years to understand the real implications of what they had to say about the shape of faith's new age, but I remember reading the books with a huge sense of relief and liberation. They were among the things that compelled me to ask for a sabbatical year in order to think about my life in a religious order. In fact, they were part of a revolution in my life, which led me eventually to the Society of Friends.

When I wrote *The World in my Heart* I was even more sharply aware of the fact that old ways of expressing faith and envisaging God were breaking down and that we were on the edge of something new. I was rather flippant about it because I was afraid of letting go of the old, frightened of all the unknown possibilities of the 'new'. To let go of those things in the Christian tradition that had given me a sense of security was quite frightening at that point. John Robinson wrote about the end of theism, that is, the God who is over and above us, the God 'out there'. But I still talked away to a God who was not simply an inward reality. If God is somehow the Ground of everything that is, and intimately connected with the evolutionary story, then perhaps my urgent S.O.S. is still received, or perhaps I am simply reconnected to the power within myself.

I remember that 40 years ago I was feeling very much as many people in the churches are feeling today – that traditional ways of expressing faith and of envisaging the divine have failed to make any sense. Today we are even more aware that the 'old' has come to an end. We know that we are on the edge of the new, but we sense it as an unknown territory still, unmapped and, therefore, with no familiar landmarks. It takes courage to be in a place like that. There may also be a painful sense of bereavement that something that was once so precious to us has died and cannot be called back.

During the last decade of the twentieth century and the beginning of this century, a number of reports and surveys of contemporary British Quakerism, Swarthmore Lectures, and research by Quaker scholars have documented the uncertainty and confusion of many Friends when it comes to being articulate about their faith. Others have deplored the extremes of spiritual anarchy, which have enabled Friends to produce their own individual versions of Quaker spirituality. In 1980 the Quaker study centre Woodbrooke published an essay by Joan Fitch – 'The Present Tense', in which she attempted to find out why contemporary Friends seemed unable to be articulate about their faith.

John Punshon in his 1990 Swarthmore Lecture *Testimony and Tradition* lamented the fact that contemporary Quakerism was, in his words, 'supermarket Quakerism'.[3] He saw us shopping around and picking from the shelves whatever took our fancy, to make our own 'pick-and-mix' brand of spirituality. This comment caused me some amusement since that is exactly what George Fox did in selecting the kind of worship and the particular practices and emphases that were to become characteristic of early Quakerism.

In an analysis of the state of the Society of Friends in Britain, Alastair Heron deplored what he called 'a secular and humanist trend' that he believed reflected a lack of spiritual experience.[4] Bonhoeffer, presumably, would have welcomed the secular, humanist trend as a sign of the 'religionless Christianity' he believed would characterise our coming of age. And I am far from convinced that anyone of us is in a position to comment or speculate on the 'personal spiritual experience' of others. Indeed George Fox, in a pastoral letter, warned Friends about any attempts to judge one another.[5]

In the 1994 Swarthmore Lecture, Margaret Heathfield posed the question as to whether or not we wanted to be 'a people of God' rather than an 'open spiritual movement' and warned Friends: 'We may not be able to continue indefinitely to keep all our options open. We may be forced to choose.'[6] In a similar vein Jonathan Dale suggested that we ought not to be contented with what he saw as the highly 'individualistic, relativistic and fragmented Quakerism of this time'. He saw it as 'weakening our corporate life' and 'undermining our confidence in our coherence'.[7]

Some researchers and writers on contemporary Quaker life see a culture of openness and diversity as something to be lamented rather than celebrated, suggesting that our desire as

---

[3] *Testimony and Tradition*, p. 23. [4] *Our Quaker Tradition*, p. 33.
[5] Epistle 48; *No more but my love*, p. 22.
[6] *Being Together*, pp. 87–88. [7] *Beyond the Spirit of the Age*, p. 121.

0

0

Friends to be an open community creates uncertainty about what we are and who we are. Britain Yearly Meeting's *Quaker News* has echoed this: 'We live in a time which could be described as Quaker uncertainty or confusion: in a Yearly Meeting of many differences, particularly differently expressed beliefs, but also varied perceptions of what we should be about as Friends.'[8]

I do not think we should discount these critiques of contemporary Quaker life. What they say needs to be taken seriously. They are describing what they see taking place within Britain Yearly Meeting. However, my own interpretation of this confusion, uncertainty and diversity is rather different. Some of these surveys appear to imply that Friends are somehow 'not good enough', that we have lost any sense of divine imperative, are lacking in discipline, or in a proper understanding of the Quaker way. Or they look at the present situation in which Friends seem to be so uncertain and confused, so inclined to individualism, and so diverse, and see these as symptoms of a malaise that is liable to bring about the demise of the Society of Friends.

In many ways all these historical researches and surveys of our contemporary spirituality seem to me to be looking backwards and making comparisons between contemporary and seventeenth-century Friends. They appear to assume that there was once a 'golden age' of Quakerism in which we were all in unity, spoke with a corporate compelling voice and possessed an agreed understanding of what it means to be a Quaker. Any serious study of Quaker history, particularly during the first period of it, ought to disabuse us on that score. It also seems very odd to me that the beginnings of anything should be regarded as the norm. If this were so, for example, in the case of medicine and health care, I would not be alive today.

These surveys also seem to assume that secularism and individualism are somehow to be deplored. The latter I find amusing since if there were a prize awarded to the most ardent Quaker individualist of all time it would surely go to George Fox! We find it quite satisfactory to agree with William Penn in his assessment of Fox as 'no man's copy',[9] but find it disconcerting when the Society of Friends produces a bumper crop of individualists.

8 *Quaker News* no. 23.

1. On the Edge of the New

It seems proper to these critics of our contemporary individualism to assume that the very beginnings of our Quaker story offer a model for us today but they seem to forget that the early Quaker movement was characterised by a passionate individualism. Larry Ingle observes that Fox's interpretation of his experiences made it almost inevitable that the test of authentic faith should be 'each person's private encounter with God'.[10] Indeed the Society of Friends has had to live the contradiction between George Fox's impassioned invitation to a spirituality based on individual experience, and his exhortations to Friends not to 'go beyond their measure'[11] and later his attempts to formalise and impose order on his runaway movement.

More worrying to me is the fact that none of the writers of these serious studies of contemporary Quaker life seem to be aware of the enormous 'God Shift' and spiritual paradigm shifts that were a feature of our twentieth century, and now of our twenty-first-century life. If they were aware they might be thankful that we seem to be 'an open spiritual movement'. For although over 90 per cent of the population in this country has voted with their feet against formal religious affiliation there is evidence that many of those who have 'opted out' continue to have a lively interest in spirituality.

In his broadcast talks Gerald Priestland expressed the view that our western world was becoming less and less religious, but more and more spiritual. He received thousands of letters from listeners who had no connection with formal religion but saw themselves on a spiritual journey. I remember that the mainstream churches were so encouraged by his observations (though they failed to take the real point of them) that they set up the 'decade of evangelism' in what proved, not surprisingly, to be an unsuccessful attempt to bring 'home' these spiritual 'outsiders'.

Two former Anglican nuns, Hannah Ward and Jennifer Wild, have written a book in which they suggest that there are many of us who no longer feel entirely at home in the formal religious institutions. They ask 'Is all this the beginning of the end of Christianity, or could it be the work of the Holy Spirit?' They see what is happening as a sign of the times, that things are coming to an end and that we are on the edge of something new.

[9] Preface to Fox's *Journal*, ed. Nickalls, p. xliii. [10] *First among Friends*, p. 52. [11] Epistle 118; in *No More but My Love*, p. 50.

They go on to describe the experience of many contemporary Christians as a real wilderness state, a sense of having grown out of, or away from, old belief systems and forms of worship. 'We experience the present as barren and bewildering; the old has died but the new is beyond our grasp.'[12]

The main argument of their book is that those who are aware of having moved away from traditional ways of being a community of faith or who are on the fringes of the institutional churches are not necessarily unfaithful doubters who represent a pastoral problem. Rather, they suggest, they may well be people who have been called into the wilderness to discover new ways of being faith communities. I found this book refreshing because it describes so clearly the experience of many of us. They suggest that we are 'boundary-dwellers'; not 'marginal' or 'spiritual anarchists', but rather people of faith who are on the boundary between two worlds, the old and the yet-to-be. Far from being something negative they point out that in different religions this time of being 'betwixt and between' has been considered to be a sacred time. They quote the anthropologist Arnold Gennep, who describes such experiences and times as 'liminal', from the Latin word limen meaning threshold. He explains in his writings that the liminal period of any rite of passage is, in fact, the most sacred and intense period.

I remember being one of the participants in the follow-up to the First International Theological Conference for Quaker Women (which had been held at Woodbrooke in 1991), hearing Zoë White speak about her debt to those within the Judaic-Christian tradition who had become outsiders, people who had dared to stand at the very edge of the tradition, refusing the conventional or safe ways of being part of it. She described them as 'Desert People' and went on to say that in order to be part of a new exodus we have to 'be willing to enter the desert – to feel "deserted by the known"'... As Desert People, we need to find the courage to honour our confusion, and in Carter Heywood's words to live "patiently in the dialectic between confusion and clarity...".'[13]

Similarly, John Shelby Spong, former Bishop of Newark, New Jersey and best selling author of a number of books about

[12] *Guard the Chaos*, Introduction. [13] *Living Faithfully with Passion*, pp. 10–11.

the end of the old, has chosen to call himself 'a believer in exile' and notes that from the thousands of letters he receives it seems clear to him that there are many people of faith like him, who also feel themselves to be 'in exile'. Some of them have moved out of the faith communities in which they have been nurtured and now feel themselves both unnurtured and alienated. Others are hanging on by the skin of their teeth, but also are feeling unsustained.

He compares our sense of being 'believers in exile' to that of the Jews deported to Babylon in the sixth century BCE. They did not expect to see their homeland again. The Temple, which for them was God's earthly dwelling place, had been desecrated and finally destroyed. Jerusalem, their holy city, was a heap of rubble. Their nationhood was destroyed along with the devastation of their land. All their familiar religious rituals and customs were lost to them. All that had given their lives meaning, as people chosen by God, had been eroded. The sacred story that told them how God had given them this land was meaningless, its meaning destroyed as the land was laid waste. The festivals, which traditionally had been celebrated in Jerusalem, could never be celebrated there again. The whole fabric of their religious lives was torn out of the context in which it had been woven. Taunted by their captors 'Sing us one of the songs of Zion,' they could only respond 'How could we sing the Lord's song in a foreign land?'[14]

Spong goes on to point out that in exile the Jewish people in the sixth century BCE were forced to abandon all their traditional ideas about God, all the assumptions they had made, all their preconceptions. And he insists that our exile has done the same for us. 'The Jewish people could not return to the good old days. Neither can believers in this generation ... The God content of the past no longer sustains the contemporary spirit'.[15] Eventually, however, the exile came to an end and for some, at least, there was a return to their devastated homeland, but their old ideas about God had undergone a sea change.

I can remember very clearly that I felt rather like that when I left the Order of Deaconesses in the Methodist Church and

---

[14] Psalms 137:4 (New Revised Standard Version). [15] *Why Christianity Must Change or Die*, p. 41.

found my way into the Quaker community. At first it was very like the way in which Gerald Priestland described his experience of coming among Friends. It felt like 'coming home'. But in spite of feeling at home among Friends my ideas of God had undergone a similar kind of sea change and eventually I felt a sense of loss for some of the things I had left behind. And 'being at home' didn't mean that the questioning mind and spirit that had brought me to Friends was put to sleep or fell away because I had somehow found the Holy Grail.

There are Friends who seem to think that it should be like that. They seem to believe that the Quaker Way represents God's last and most satisfactory experiment in creating a faith community. They understand that people in the mainstream churches may well feel that traditional ways of worship and expressions of faith no longer speak to them. After all, this is why many of us have come away from those churches to find a more satisfying spiritual home amongst Quakers. But they assume that we have no need to take part in the kinds of radical reappraisal that are going on in some of the mainstream churches, and particularly among many theologians, and people in religious orders.

When I think of the wider Quaker community in Britain, particularly in our institutional aspect, it has gradually become clear to me that we are not free of many of the traditional God concepts. Behind or underlying many of the things we do are pictures of God that belonged to the mediaeval worldview. George Fox, for example, clearly believed in a God of Wrath, and was keen to consign those who did not agree with him, or whose behaviour seemed reprehensible, to 'the lake of fire'. Knowing nothing about viruses or the probable causes of infection he, and many of his contemporaries, saw the plagues which devastated the population of Europe from the mid-fifteenth to the mid-seventeenth century as a clear sign of God's extreme anger.

This sense of being under the judgement of a powerful and implacable God was no doubt responsible for the adolescent depression of someone like George Fox, and also for the hellfire sermons he delivered in an attempt to persuade people to turn away from their wrongdoing and lead blameless lives. No doubt the bleak heritage of Calvinistic predetermination also contributed to his sense that nothing would avert the wrath of

God except, possibly, lives of extraordinary holiness.

His picture of God was still essentially a medieval one, in the sense that it was profoundly monarchical. One of his favourite phrases was 'The Power of God is over all'. For him, God was supreme judge and cosmic ruler, who demanded total obedience and submission to his will. Indeed these undergird the way we worship and the way we conduct our church affairs. In them we claim that we are there to listen to the inward promptings of the Spirit and to discover and be obedient to the will of God. Today there have been many feminist critiques of the monarchical models of God.

George Fox believed that the biblical story of creation was not a myth but a genuine cosmology, a description of the perfect world created by God and then spoiled by human disobedience. In one of the best known of his 'Openings', when he described his experience of creation being open to him,[16] he believed that he had been transported back to Eden and was now in the sinless state of Adam before the Fall and could walk and talk with God as Adam had done.

Today we have a quite different cosmology that arises from what we know now about the origin of the universe. We know that the universe has a story, a history reaching back some thirteen billion years or more, that it is immeasurably vaster than our minds can grasp, and that it is still in the process of expanding and developing. The universe story is our story even though, relatively speaking, we have only just stepped onto the stage. We are not, as the old story told us, the fallen children of Eve, living in a world that was once perfect and is now flawed and corrupted by human sin. The new story tells us that we are only evolutionary toddlers in this vast and mind-blowing cosmic scenario. We are unfinished beings, still learning by trial and error, what it might mean to be fully human.

In her talk to the members of the Quaker Lesbian and Gay Fellowship at their annual conference in 1993, Zoë White spoke of how much she had been helped by words of Bishop Richard Holloway, when he said in a conference she had been attending, 'All our thinking about God is provisional and discardable'. She went on to say that he encouraged the participants to think in

16 *Journal*, ed. Nickalls, p. 27.

31

terms of a God of the provisional:

> meaning that we have to be willing to be experimental, to confront and throw away all the names for God, and ways and systems we have used to replace God – anything in fact which has become fixed or fossilised, which has become idolatrous. And we have to be willing to wait, in silent vulnerable openness of spirit for the new word, the new revelation that will come in God's time.[17]

In his 1965 Swarthmore Lecture John MacMurray suggested that we should begin to create a new kind of theology, 'empirical in temper, checking theory against contemporary experience, religious and scientific. It should be freely critical of the past, recognising that in this field of knowledge as in others antiquity is no indication of validity ... It should be concerned to reject openly and explicitly what it can no longer accept, and it should not expect nor too eagerly desire unanimity'.[18]

Janet Scott took up the challenge in her 1980 Swarthmore Lecture *What Canst Thou Say?* and invited Friends to explore different models of God and to regard all ways of doing theology, talking about God and faith, as provisional and inadequate. She suggested that all such exploration should take into account current knowledge of science and other contemporary disciplines. Her lecture marked one of the first clear recognitions that traditional ways of understanding faith, including Quaker ways, needed to be reviewed in the light of new knowledge. It prepared the way for doing theology in the light of our awareness of being on the edge of a new age.

In 1942 Etty Hillesum, a Jewish student and teacher, wrote in her diary 'there is only one way of preparing the new age, by living it now in our hearts ... I would so much like to help prepare the new age'.[19] She died in Auschwitz in November 1943. We have written this book in the hope that it will help us, and many other Friends, to live the new age, by living it now in our hearts.

---

[17] *Preparing the New Age*, pp. 10–11. [18] *The Search for Reality in Religion*, 1995 ed., p. 73. [19] Quoted by Zoë White in the Introduction to *Preparing the New Age*.

Chapter 2
Living Between Stories

Alex Wildwood

The great interest in spirituality today stems in part from the general awareness that we live on a planet torn apart by much suffering and violence. ... A profound crisis of meaning has arisen whose roots can be traced to a loss of vision, commitment, and faith – what is in fact a deep spiritual crisis. An immense spiritual hunger exists to find a life of deeper significance than that of material goods, consumerism, and exploitative capitalism.

Ursula King[1]

We are talking about a religious crisis and a religious opportunity, a spiritual awakening that is far more demanding than the Reformation times of the sixteenth century.

Matthew Fox[2]

When I first started collaborating on this text with Jo I found myself surprised by how deeply she is rooted in the biblical stories which clearly were formative for her. I belong to a generation for whom the importance of this biblical worldview and its theology had already greatly diminished. For myself, Bible texts have (sadly) far too many negative connotations of rote learning and the insensitive imposition of doctrinal religion.

In my local Quaker meeting we lack a shared sense of how (or even whether) to introduce our children to Bible stories, which have, for most of us, long since lost any sense of God-given authority. Even as sources of life-wisdom, they seem archaic and

[1] *The Search for Spirituality*, p. ix. [2] 'Spirituality for a new era', p. 201.

contradictory to most modern readers, coming as they do from such a different era and culture. Yet few of us would want to abandon them completely – and I for one am glad for fresh approaches which try to bring the texts to life for readers today.[3] The fact that the Bible sits on the meeting house table, a source of inspiration for some older Friends but an artefact speaking of a distant past for many of us, reminds me that Thomas Berry suggested we have a moratorium on written scriptures while we learnt to study the natural world, which he called 'the primary revelation of the divine'. Maybe that shift is part of what's happening right now, as we take stock of the stories that have traditionally given meaning to our lives and take part in creating new ones.

My own religious influences and experiences have been more eclectic than Jo's. Our two voices reflect something of the diversity of contemporary ways of talking about the divine found amongst British Quakers today, and also reflect the theological challenge of these times, when we must often translate one another's religious language and learn to negotiate a multiplicity of ways of expressing our faith. I too identify as what John Shelby Spong calls 'a believer in exile'[4] – and recognise that this involves a willingness to let go of what has been; a need to trust and open to what is beyond the comfort of the familiar and the known. As the novelist Nadine Gordimer observes, 'An interim period is a vulnerable one; the old is not yet old enough to have fully died away and the new is yet too young to have been born.'[5]

At times I feel a real split within myself. On the one hand I am clearly a Quaker, I identify strongly as such and have been in membership of the Religious Society of Friends for over two decades. I feel I belong here, that this is my community of faith. I'm comfortable with Friends' ways and understand our particular jargon and idiosyncrasies. Yet I find myself in the strange position of being unable to describe myself as any kind of Christian,

[3] For instance, *Friendly Bible Study* by Joanne & Larry Spears; *Engaging Scripture: reading the Bible with Early Friends*, by Michael L. Birkel; *Reading the Bible again for the first time: taking the Bible seriously but not literally*, by Marcus J. Borg. [4] See his book *Why Christianity Must Change or Die: A bishop speaks to believers in exile.* [5] Quoted by John O'Donohue in "The Priestliness of the Human Heart" pp. 43–53.

while feeling that I was led amongst Friends, a religious body whose historic and inspirational foundations lie unmistakably within the Christian mystical tradition.[6] The broad spiritual influences that have shaped me, and the threats to our planet which for me must form the context to any meaningful theological speculation today, both call me to a greater identity. They remind me that our denominational affiliations are little more than tribal loyalties, something with which we must sit lightly if we are to identify with the greater reality, the 'body' to which we truly belong.

At its inception, the Quaker movement was a reaction to the dead formalism of organised church religion, an encouragement to trust the inward light of divine guidance available to each person. Emphasising the Inward Light (the Inner Guide or Teacher) made external forms – the priests and doctrines, the hymns and set prayers of traditional religious worship – redundant. At its heart was the radical faith that no human intermediaries were necessary for someone to experience communion with their God. The early Quaker movement grew out of a community of seekers waiting in silence because the old religious forms no longer served them, were felt to be inadequate. They sought instead immediate divine guidance as the basis for individual and community decision-making.

Today a growing number of British Quakers make no reference to our Christian roots; they have left behind not only the outward forms but also the inward reference points of Christian faith. The underlying theology of our Quaker worship and witness no longer makes sense to them. A dear F/friend once said to me (when I attempted to describe my perception of the divine in what for him were clearly hopelessly nebulous terms) 'But, Alex, does your God have a will?' Like a growing number of Friends in Britain today I question the assumptions implicit in that theological formulation. My own sense of the divine is less personal than the God of Christian belief; yet I am a Friend because I do believe we may be led when in worship or quiet reflection we attend to 'the promptings of love and truth' in the heart, and we 'Trust them as the leadings of God whose Light shows us our darkness and brings us to new life.'[7]

[6] See my chapters in *Rooted in Christianity, Open to New Light.*
[7] *Advices & Queries* 1.

Some years ago now my father-in-law was driving to an important meeting at work and commented to his then 14-year-old daughter that he felt like Daniel entering the lion's den. 'Who's Daniel?' she replied. This anecdote speaks of how we may no longer assume a common religious story today – especially across the generations. Even as someone who does not turn to the Bible for inspiration or guidance I find this disconcerting because much of our shared cultural life rests – like my father-in-law's allusion – on the common currency of these tales. Whether we think them 'true' or not, the loss of this common cultural and religious language is part of the uncertainty of our age.

For the vast majority of people in the Western world today the traditional, biblical worldview neither fires the imagination nor satisfies our souls. In the late nineteenth and early twentieth centuries Biblical texts began to lose their authority as they were increasingly shown to be inconsistent with emerging scientific accounts of our human and planetary origins. The concern then was whether these stories were 'true', whether they were an accurate account of what actually happened. Biblical scholarship and analysis – together with archaeological discoveries and evidence from a growing number of scientific disciplines – began to undermine the explanatory power of these traditional accounts.

Elsewhere[8] I have outlined the reasons for this loss of biblical faith in terms of the intellectual revolutions in Europe from the seventeenth century to the present day, how developments in astronomy, geology, evolutionary biology, and in the twentieth century, psychology and quantum physics, all contributed to undermining the biblical worldview, and ultimately the power and influence of church religion.

Today, many of us accept Bible stories as amalgamations of history, legend and myth; the question for us is not 'Are they true?' but 'Do they satisfy us?' Do they meet our human need for an account of our human origins and purpose? Do they offer us a story that can inspire and challenge us as we address both our everyday concerns as well as the global situation in which we now find ourselves? Dramatically declining church attendance (in most denominations) and growing indifference to doctrinal faith (especially among the young) suggest they no longer do.

8 In *Tradition & Transition.*

2. Living Between Stories

Since the 1970s when Gerald Priestland made the observation that people in the West were becoming 'less and less religious and more and more spiritual', that trend has become even more apparent. The 'Soul of Britain' survey conducted by the BBC in 2000 identified how, even as church attendance continues to decline in this country, 'more than 76% of the population would admit to having had a spiritual experience.' In hardly more than a decade they found 'there has been a 59 per cent rise in the positive response rate to questions about this subject. Compared with 25 years ago, the rise is greater than 110 per cent.'[9] It seems that we have entered a new era, one characterised by what Australian sociologist David Tacey has named 'the spirituality revolution'. Spirituality, he suggests, now refers to 'our relationship to the sacredness of life, nature, and the universe, and this relationship is no longer felt to be confined to formal devotional practice or to institutional places of worship'.[10]

This significant social phenomenon has happened both very rapidly and very recently in historical terms, and all of us – both inside and outside traditional faith communities – are still adjusting to this new reality. But this seismic shift in religious culture has enabled people of my generation to express a sense of spiritual curiosity; it has given us a freedom to explore the religious life, undreamt of by our parents or grandparents. Today, the monopoly that Christian religion once claimed on the spiritual imagination of people in the West has been broken open and the waters of the Spirit are bubbling up all over the place. As Jo says in Chapter 1, this radical questioning of previous convictions is not confined to any one denomination or faith tradition. Rather, it is a characteristic of this time, that permeates all aspects of our cultural life.

But while spirituality is increasingly contrasted with religion, it is important not to set up a simplistic dichotomy between the two. For feminist theologian Nicola Slee, 'The spiritual can be distinguished from the religious and understood as something wider than religiosity; on the other hand, it can be understood as the deepest and most central element of religion.'[11] Ursula King, professor of theology and religious studies at Bristol University,

---

[9] David Hay & Kate Hunt, 'Is Britain's soul waking up?'
[10] *The Spirituality Revolution*, p. 38. [11] *Faith & Feminism*, p. 95.

cautions us all to take a broad approach at this time: 'Such a sharp separation between spirituality and religion is not helpful for the development of the personal and social transformations so urgently needed if greater flourishing of humans and the earth is to be achieved around the globe.'[12]

Nevertheless, the widespread questioning of religious authority and tradition, the demand by many people today to know things of the spirit experientially, quite precisely defines the exciting historical moment in which we live. Today growing numbers of people feel free to experiment and choose what works for them; they are applying to spiritual exploration the same kind of questioning and pragmatic testing that are characteristic of the scientific method.

Of course, there are those who decry this new pluralism, who fear the loss of what is familiar in their faith, who want to squeeze the postmodern genie back into the lamp of biblical tradition. They deplore what they see as syncretism, the mixing and merging of different faiths. Yet the briefest delving into history shows that this is precisely how religious traditions evolve – by incorporating and adjusting to cultural infusion and exchange. We don't need to believe that Jesus was literally born in December to appreciate how the pre-Christian festival of the Winter Solstice in northern Europe suited the theme of rebirth and renewal that for Christians the season signifies.

The new reality is that while Christianity still claims a privileged role in the educational and ceremonial life of our nation (we remain a nominally Christian culture), for the vast majority of the population church religion is now simply an irrelevance.[13] Within scarcely more than one generation, we have witnessed what social historian Callum Brown has characterised in the title of his study as 'the death of Christian Britain'. In a remarkably short space of time, the yoke of religious orthodoxy has been cast off – and the fear, guilt and social control which for millions of people have been its hallmarks.

Brown challenges the conventional wisdom of a gradual process of creeping secularisation since the mid-nineteenth cen-

12 *The Search for Spirituality*, p. 2.
13 See the section on 'Cultural Change' in Linda Murgatroyd's essay 'The Future of Quakers in Britain'.

tury; his research points to a sudden, dramatic collapse of church attendance and affiliation in the 1960s. During this decade, he argues, women 'cancelled their mass subscription' to the church of their mothers as part of their radical questioning of the nature of feminine identity. (I discuss more fully Callum Brown's thesis, and the relationship between declining church congregations and the rise of 'the new spirituality' and the impact this has had on British Friends, in *Rooted in Christianity, Open to New Light* Chapter 3, 'Mapping our diversity'.)

Like many of my contemporaries I am excited by this shift in spiritual consciousness, to be alive in a time pregnant with possibility, which reflects how an economically and geographically mobile, educated population is seeking new ways of sensing the sacred, and being drawn to experiential ways of reaching for transcendence. David Tacey calls this 'the Spirituality Revolution'; to Robert Forman it is 'grassroots spirituality' (his book title); William Bloom writes of 'holistic spirituality' and offers this definition: 'Spirituality: The natural human connection with the wonder and energy of nature, cosmos and all existence; and the instinct to explore and understand its meaning.'[14] Today, bookshops in every city of the land offer huge selections of 'Mind/Body/Spirit' titles, where all faiths and wisdom traditions are represented. The ready availability of such titles is also a new reality, an important aspect of this time of transition. Robert Forman, professor of comparative religions at Hunter College, New York, notes: 'There has never before been an era in which every single major religious tradition is readily available to any educated person'.[15]

The growing self-identification of many people in the West as 'spiritual but not religious', the marked overall decline in church attendance and membership in the past forty years, people's growing confidence in speaking about their experiences of the numinous (with or without using 'God' language) all evidence the shift I am describing. There is also a reclaiming of the word 'soul' – which is associated with depth, darkness and earthiness – as opposed to 'spirit' which is linked with light, ascension and the element of air. Thomas Moore, author of several

[14] www.f4hs.org/ and see also *Soulution: the holistic manifesto*.
[15] *Grassroots Spirituality*, p. 122.

bestselling books on the subject, speaks of caring for the soul by
'cultivating a richly expressive and meaningful life at home and
in society'[16] – and of how this may be done without reference to
organised religion or spiritual practice per se.[17]

The contemporary blossoming of spirituality can be seen in
the widespread interest in making retreats, as witnessed by the
popularity of the BBC television series 'The Monastery' and 'The
Monastery Revisited' transmitted in the UK in 2005–6; the for-
mat gave rise to further BBC documentaries 'The Retreat', 2007
(following Islamic retreatants) and 'The Convent', 2009.[18] Meditation and yoga classes are readily available in most towns and
cities in Britain today: see for instance Paul Heelas and Linda
Woodhead, *The Spiritual Revolution: Why religion is giving way to
spirituality* – a fascinating study of change in the rural community
of Kendal, Cumbria. There has been a veritable explosion of
the 'Mind/Body/Spirit' category on publishers' lists. All these
phenomena suggest that a growing number of spiritual seekers are looking for something they are not finding in conventional congregations of belief. Best-selling non-fiction titles of
the past three decades have included a number of 'spiritual-but-
not-religious' books: for example, M. Scott Peck, *The Road Less
Travelled*; Deepak Chopra, *How to Know God*; Eckhart Tolle, *The
Power of Now*; and the Conversations with God series of books
'channelled' by Neale Donald Walsch; all these titles can be have
found in meeting house libraries or have been cited by Friends
and attenders as influential.

This contemporary 'unaffiliated' spirituality emphasises
both solo practices such as meditation and developing mind-
fulness (with a deliberate blurring of distinctions between
'personal growth' and spiritual practice) and small, spiritual self-
help groups. Such groups have arisen, Robert Forman suggests,
as 'both an answer to our spiritual hunger and a response to the
loneliness of a mobile and impersonal society'.[19] Being both self-

[16] *Care of the Soul*, p. 4; see also his other books in the bibliography.
[17] See, for instance, *The Quest: Exploring a sense of soul*, as an example of the broadening of the search for meaning and purpose in
everyday life and relationships. Joycelin Dawes, its lead author, is a
Quaker. [18] See also Finding Sanctuary, by Abbot Christopher Jamison (who featured in 'The Monastery') which received widespread
critical acclaim. [19] *Grassroots Spirituality*, p. 65.

organising and leaderless in the traditional sense (leadership as a function being shared between participants) 'neither the size, breadth, nor importance of what is going on has been generally grasped',[20] and in its emphasis on 'relationship, human contact, exploration and interpersonal support – the spiritual world is now highly shaped by a feminine sensibility'.[21] This is a great shift from the centuries of being led by 'distant, sometimes intimidating priests, rabbis, ministers, gurus, and community shamans … In our new willingness to each discover our own path, articulate our own insights, and in our ability to help each other, we have learned to sound the spiritual depths without relying on some mediating hierarchical authorities.'[22]

In its style of peer support groups, its mode of intimate sharing of personal experience and the refusal to separate the spiritual and the emotional, the sacred and the bodily, the impact of women's experience and styles of relating have been profound, and this links, of course, with Callum Brown's observation that it was women's disaffiliation from the church that was pivotal to the sudden dramatic decline of its influence and authority since the nineteen-sixties.

With their emphasis on a feeling-centred small group process where people share their lives in an intimate way, intuitively reaching to their deepest values, these new forms of spiritual exploration owe much to women's consciousness-raising groups of the nineteen-sixties and seventies. Although this style of small, self-led spiritual support and study groups can be found both within and beyond the churches, not surprisingly, this spiritual movement is most apparent on the margins of the mainstream. Matthew Fox (who describes himself as a post-denominational priest)[23] sees young people being drawn to new forms of spirituality precisely because 'the faith traditions of their birth have failed to teach them mystical practice and a mystical inheritance'. 'New Age' practices and the wider spirituality movement I am describing have become refuges for those 'feeling a call to experience Divinity instead of just hearing about God or about God's commandments',[24] and he observes that today, 'There are

---

[20] *Ibid.*, p. 2. [21] *Ibid.*, p. 115. [22] *Ibid.*, p. 66. [23] In the title of his book, *Confessions: The making of a post-denominational priest.*
[24] 'Spirituality for a new era', p. 197.

far more people wounded by the church, feeling deserted by the church, or simply fed up with the lack of spiritual nourishment from church than there are those going to church.'[25]

While I share an enthusiasm for this sense of an experimental, exploratory spirituality, other commentators point to shortcomings in the rise of 'spirituality' as individualistic and compromised by commercialism. In *Selling Spirituality*, Jeremy Carrette and Richard King argue that spirituality has become a powerful commodity in the global market place and that the 'privatisation' of religion simply reflects how the 'market mentality' has infiltrated all aspects of human cultural expression in the West. Clearly, market forces can – and will – turn anything into a commodity in our consumer culture. Ursula King comments that 'a superficial consumerist approach takes away much of the vibrant aspects and depths of what spirituality is about ... a spirituality exclusively focused on personal concerns such as finding inner peace, one's true self, or a purpose in life – however valuable for the individual – can produce a rather escapist attitude'.[26]

Yet for all these shortcomings, a significant social movement is underway; increasing numbers of people are exploring for themselves what psychologist and former minister David Elkins describes as 'alternative paths to the sacred'; they are moving (as the title of his book has it) 'Beyond Religion', realising that spiritual development 'is not about religious rituals and practices; it is about waking up to the wonder of life'.[27] William Bloom, an articulate and impassioned proponent of 'holistic spirituality', defines spirituality as the 'natural human connection with the wonder and energy of nature, cosmos and all existence; and the instinct to explore and understand its meaning'.[28]

On the one hand what has been dubbed the 'new spirituality' is an improvisation, a creative reaction to the failure of doctrinal religion to satisfy the spiritual needs of many people today; on the other the movement is part of something ever greater, one aspect of a broader cultural shift in consciousness occurring at this time. New understandings of the nature of reality given to us by science actually enhance a sense of the mysteriousness of

---

[25] *Ibid.*, p. 198. [26] *The Search for spirituality*, p. 11. [27] *Beyond Religion*, p. 4. [28] www.f4hs.org – and see also his book *The Power of Modern Spirituality*.

existence. A number of works in recent decades have addressed the way in which new understandings of the nature of reality, coming from physicists especially, are taking scientists into territory traditionally considered the province of religion – for instance Fritjof Capra, *The Tao of Physics*; Fritjof Capra & David Steindl-Rast, *Belonging to the Universe*; Paul Davies, *The mind of God*; Diarmuid O'Murchu, *Quantum Theology*; Peter Russell, *From science to God*; Gary Kowalski, *Science and the search for God*; Ervin Laszlo, *Science & the re-enchantment of the Cosmos*.

An emerging new awareness of our origins, an awesome sense of the vastness of the universe we inhabit, of the strangeness of matter at the subatomic level, and a profound appreciation of the intrinsic relatedness of all exists – in a word a new cosmology – is changing, for many of us, how we imagine and relate to Ultimate Reality and must, inevitably, influence how we define and practise the spiritual life. This new story of our origins also suggests a new understanding of revelation itself – not as the occasional self-disclosure of a totally-other Creator, but as 'new awareness of how the ultimate mysteries of existence are being manifest in the universe about us'.[29]

For a growing number of us today, scientific discoveries and observations necessarily inform our sense of spirituality – even while we are aware of the dangers of what theologian John Haught calls 'the belief system of scientific materialism … the idea that deadness is the ultimate origin and destiny of all being'.[30] Just as many of us can no longer feel at home in traditional faith congregations, we also want to challenge the assumptions of mechanistic science and the limitations of humanism – sensing as we do that both these approaches reduce the awesome wonder of the world we inhabit.

There is a further, sobering dimension to this shift in spiritual awareness in this time. I am of a generation who realised we are heirs to a truly terrible legacy. My father worked for the American Air Force and his particular responsibility was 'Ground Safety', everything from drunken driving by airmen to the safety of nuclear bombers when they were on the ground. I remember catching sight of manuals showing the effects on buildings of

[29] Thomas Berry & Brian Swimme, *The Universe Story*, p. 223.
[30] See article by Carter Phipps, 'A theologian of renewal'.

early atomic tests. While confidently schooled in a worldview that believed in the inevitability of progress, I was also growing with an awareness of how science and technology can be used with horrifying effect to amplify human destructiveness. Some years later, while I was at university, the modern environmental movement was born. To the awareness of the awesome destructiveness of modern weaponry was added a growing realisation that 'we' (the industrialised nations of the world) were effectively at war with nature itself.

This has to be the proper context to the contemporary quest for a meaningful spirituality; the urgent need to create a new form of human presence on this planet. We are at an evolutionary break-point and all of us share (at some level of awareness) a responsibility so painful that as a culture we are, understandably, perfecting the arts of denial and self-distraction. For the almost unbearable truth is that we are confronted today by what Susan Griffin calls 'a staggering observation, difficult to take in: human society is destroying life on earth'. Faced with this reality, she writes, 'yet another terrain seems to vanish too ... ways in which the world made sense and heaven and earth were connected into one pattern of meaning'. That is how uncomfortable it should feel to be alive with awareness today. At such a time of disintegration, of course people are fearful and uncertain. Yet an enormous potential also beckons today when, in Susan Griffin's words, 'the understanding that nature is a source of meaning encounters the hope for a just society'.[31]

At such a time of radical uncertainty it is no surprise that we are witnessing the rise of fundamentalisms of all kinds – religious, economic or scientific – which are designed to reassure and provide certainty when doubt and change abound. Fundamentalism is, at heart, as the Chief Rabbi Jonathan Sacks puts it, 'the attempt to impose a single truth on a plural world'.[32]

I believe Thomas Berry accurately describes our 'condition' today as having 'thought to reduce the Earth to our own human dimension ... to make the Earth obedient to ourselves rather than ourselves becoming responsive to the Earth. Obviously we are not succeeding'.[33] The 'more-than-human world' is a phrase that poetically challenges the hubris of our species, used

---

31 *The Eros of Everyday Life*, pp. 5–7. 32 See 'Rabbi Jonathan Sachs on Fundamentalism' posted on YouTube by JINSIDER
33 Foreword to Cormac Cullinan, *Wild Law*, p. xi

by American philosopher and cultural ecologist David Abram in his book *The Spell of the Sensuous: Perception and Language in a More-than-Human World*. Cormac Cullinan, a white South African lawyer, draws an illuminating parallel for our domineering relationship towards the 'more-than-human world' as apartheid, the 'apartness' with which we think of the greater economy of life on Earth:

> The dominant cultures in our worlds are as convinced of the superiority of our species over others and of our right to rule the planet as most white South Africans once were about their right to oppress other South Africans. However, reality is once more intruding.[34]

What he calls 'the core falsehood' of our worldview is the belief that we humans are separate from the environment and that our well-being depends on exploiting the Earth.[35]

The challenges we face, the full dimensions of the perceptual shift which humanity needs to make if the diversity of life on Earth is to continue and flourish, is what Thomas Berry refers to as 'The Great Work' of our time. We need to move away from this sense of apartness to a situation where 'the human community and the living forms of Earth might now become a life-giving presence to each other'.[36] What Berry so ably articulates is that this is a religious challenge; the new spirituality movement is being born, in large part, out of a desire to reclaim our native sense of awe and wonder at the natural world, to sense again that this is literally and metaphorically the ground of our being. Yet too often our sense of relatedness and dependence on this life-sustaining matrix has actually been obstructed and obscured by religious doctrine and dogma.

What is called for in this time is a religious revisioning of ourselves and the world we inhabit. Do we yet sense in this shift a challenge to our self-awareness as great as when Kepler and Copernicus dared to suggest (and Galileo by observation demonstrated) that the Earth was not at the centre of our solar system; or when Darwin, with his theory of evolution by natural selection, helped us recognise our physical kinship with the rest of life on Earth?

[34] *Wild Law*, p. 35. [35] *Ibid.*, p. 22. [36] *The Great Work*, p. ix.

Being fully present to this time of change, feeling the enormity of the challenges we face, is calling forth new spiritual responses in this time. For some it will mean a deeper search within their given faith tradition, a reclaiming of neglected insights and teachings. For others it will mean the exploration of new forms of spiritual practice, new religious responses to our threatened world. Both within and beyond traditional faith communities it will mean a reformation of our relationship to the Earth, a reappraisal of what we consider sacred.

The Buddhist scholar and ecological activist Joanna Macy tellingly captures the evolutionary leap in human consciousness that is called for – a transformation that will need to draw on deep roots of human wisdom, knowledge and creativity:

> Now, in our time … three rivers – anguish for our world, scientific breakthroughs, and ancestral teachings – flow together. From the confluence of these rivers we drink. We awaken to what we once knew: we are alive in a living Earth, source of all we are and can achieve. Despite our conditioning by the industrial society of the last two centuries, we want to name, once again, this world as holy.[37]

Chapter 3
Speaking to Our Condition

Alex Wildwood

In the face of all the bad news, the challenge of creating a
sustainable civilisation can seem absurdly unrealistic ... Yet
it is germinating now, that sustainable society on which the
future depends. Its seeds are sprouting in countless actions
in defence of life, and in fresh perceptions of our mutual
belonging to the living body of Earth – bold, new perceptions deriving both from science and spirituality.

Joanna Macy[1]

We are crossing natural thresholds that we cannot see and
violating deadlines that we do not recognise. Nature is the
time-keeper, but we cannot see the clock.

Lester Brown[2]

It is quite common nowadays to hear a British Friend say that
such and such 'speaks to my condition' – by which they mean
'I agree wholeheartedly with that' or 'that tallies with my own
experience'. But George Fox and other early Friends used the
phrase in quite a different way. Believing that the Inward Light
revealed to them their brokenness, their inadequacies, something 'spoke to their condition' when it showed them the ways
they were falling short (the original meaning of the word sin).

As industrialised humanity we are burning a million years'
worth of fossil fuels per annum, and we are losing twenty-four

[1] *Coming Back to Life*, p. 6.
[2] *Plan B 3.0*, pp. 4–5.

billion tons of top soil every year.[3] From all sides we are presented with the evidence that human beings are now having an impact on the planet on a geological scale. There is also mounting evidence that we are currently experiencing what scientists are calling the sixth great extinction event of Earth's history. According to the fossil record, there have been only five previous periods of mass extinction in Earth's four-and-a-half billion year history; the last happened 65 million years ago and it marked the end of the Cretaceous era and the extinction of the dinosaurs. It is thought to have been caused by the impact of a giant meteorite. Today, it is the impact of human activities that are responsible for a global level of destruction.

According to recent United Nations reports, 20% of all mammal species, 12% of bird species, 20% of reptiles, 25% of amphibians, 39% of fish (mostly freshwater species) are currently threatened with extinction.[4] The evidence mounts daily that we are living in a time of crisis, at a point where we need a visionary perspective if humanity and the current diversity of life on Earth are to continue. The humbling truth is that, in Thomas Berry's haunting phrase, 'the human has become the desolation of the world'.

While people of many generations have felt that they were living in an age unlike any other, those of us now living do indeed face an unprecedented situation: never before has one single species been the cause of so much destruction – nor have they had the awareness of their own culpability. At this point in human development and in the evolution of life on Earth, we urgently need to develop a different sense of ourselves and our role in the story of the Earth. We need to take a much longer view, to see things from the perspective of what Joanna Macy calls 'deep time'.

In the process of inevitable collapse, of course, great violence is being perpetrated to maintain the unsustainable and protect the lifestyles of the globally privileged. The question is how much will remain when the economic system collapses

[3] For a detailed consideration of the impact of deforestation and the loss of top-soil, see Thom Hartmann, *The Last Hours of Ancient Sunlight*, p. 53. [4] Figures are for 2007; for updates see www.iucn/redlist.org; see also The Extinction Website: www.petermaas/nl/extinct/

completely, and how much suffering will be caused in the meantime. The ecological, social and political crises we face (including escalating conflicts and wars over ever diminishing 'natural resources')[5] are the result of an extractive economic system, based solely on ever-increasing profits and short-term economic gain. This global economic system is now taking us beyond the Earth's capacity for renewal or its ability to absorb the waste that industrialised nations produce. This is the 'Industrial Growth Society', a term Joanna Macy attributes to the Norwegian ecophilosopher Sigmund Kwaloy,[6] where human wealth is defined in terms of this rapacious of materials from the Earth to produce commodities that we are led to believe are necessary for our well-being. (The arms industry is both a key part of maintaining the inequalities of power and privilege that are key aspects of this economic system but also a blatant example of its unsustainable, violently wasteful, nature).

But this, of course, is not the whole picture. Worldwide, a revolution is underway: people on every continent are realising that we must find ways to meet our true needs without destroying the life-support systems on which we and all other species depend.[7] Globally we can see the phenomenal growth of creative, alternative ways of re-thinking our relationships with one another and with the more-than-human world: new economic models, experiments in sustainable agriculture and transport, different forms of community and family structure, a vibrant exploration of spiritual practices and body-mind healing, a growing recognition and inclusion of women's voices and experience. A global cultural revolution is underway which is arising directly in response to the state of our imperilled planet. Joanna Macy speaks of these initiatives as evidence of what she calls 'The Great Turning'.[8]

If we survive, future generations will look back on this time and see it as a critical moment in human history, an epoch in

[5] See for instance Vandana Shiva, *Water Wars: Privatization, Pollution, and Profit.* [6] *Coming Back to Life*, p. 15. [7] For broad overviews of these alternative approaches see Paul Hawken, *Blessed Unrest* and Peter Senge, *The Necessary Revolution.* See also the periodicals *Positive News*, www.positivenews.org.uk and *Permaculture Magazine*, www.permaculture.co.uk [8] See www.greatturningtimes.org for events and people exploring this conceptual approach

which decisions were made which reversed the destructiveness in which we are now caught. The most telling analogy is that of when an addict 'bottoms out', when they reach the point where they have to face reality and break through their denial, when the pain of continuing is greater than the pain of giving up the addiction.

'The Great Turning' refers to 'the epochal shift from a self-destructive industrial growth society to a life-sustaining civilization'. What is sobering in Macy's analysis though, is that our survival is not a foregone conclusion; we cannot know if this transformation in human awareness and activities will take place swiftly enough or on a large enough scale to enable complex forms of life on Earth to survive. There are those who feel we may already have reached a point of no return. James Lovelock's last two explorations of the implications of his Gaia theory point increasingly in this direction.[9]

In our busyness, in the accelerating pace of our lives in the industrial growth society, in our treatment of the more-than-human world as simply a 'resource' for human use, 'the company of our ancestors and the claims of our descendents become less and less real to us'. We are becoming, Macy suggests, 'marooned in the present'. Nuclear technologies in particular, with their almost unimaginably persistent toxic legacy 'cripple our imagination to envisage the future'.[10] From this visionary deep time perspective, Joanna Macy and colleagues were led to establish the Nuclear Guardianship Project, realising that even if we stop producing all nuclear materials today – and at the time of writing there are strong indications that the UK government intends to expand and regenerate the nuclear power industry – the existing by-products need to be guarded and safely contained for tens of thousands of years. The project envisages a future lay 'order' of disciplined women and men whose task it will be to faithfully oversee the containment of these toxic materials and tell future generations the story of how humanity risked contaminating all life on Earth through the 'poison fire' of nuclear reactivity. This project exemplifies the kind of original, creative responses that the perspective of deep time can elicit.

9 *The Revenge of Gaia: Why the Earth is fighting back – and how we can still save humanity* (2006), and *The Vanishing Face of Gaia: A final warning* (2010). 10 *Coming Back to Life*, p. 135

3. Speaking to Our Condition

Among Quakers one similarly prophetic voice is that of Marshall Massey, a biologist and member of Pacific Yearly Meeting. In *Seeking the Kingdom*, his 1989 Sunderland P. Gardner lecture to Canadian Yearly Meeting, he distinguishes three broad trends in the ecological crises of our time:[11] firstly, 'the destruction of carrying capacity' – the ability of land and sea to support life – which has extinguished great civilisations of the past. The second is 'the destruction of biological systems' – specifically, the destruction of the gene pool and the extinction of species (just three plant species – corn, wheat and rice – supply half of humanity's calories: thirty species account for 94% of our food). The third is 'the destruction of such physical buffers as are needed to make our whole planet habitable': most notably the stratospheric ozone layer and the natural balance of 'greenhouse gases' – the primary dangers of which range from severe climate shifts and coastal flooding to cancer epidemics and the extinction of innumerable wild species. The threat to our planet's oxygen 'factories' will, if not dealt with, 'literally sterilise the planet of all life except anaerobic bacteria'.[12]

As if this weren't challenging enough, Massey's prophetic analysis also identifies three special circumstances of our times: 'the extraordinary intensity of modern human demands upon the environment – due to a combination of record high populations and the global spread of the ideology of consumerism'; the 'rapid depletion of non-renewable fuels and minerals' (which we've been using to artificially boost the natural carrying capacity of our Earth)[13] and, crucially, 'the increasing distance between the daily experience of the average First World citizen, and the forces that are destroying the natural world'. Looking at those cultures which have historically reversed such destructive tendencies (though never, of course, on the global scale of our present situation) anthropologists identified 'systems of taboos protecting the environment from destruction. Religious taboos'.[14] The turnaround comes, Massey argues, from social recognition, and reinforcement, of what he simply calls 'The Sacred Order':

[11] My summary of his analysis is taken from *Seeking the Kingdom* pp. 7–9. [12] *The Defense of The Peaceable Kingdom*, p. 3. [13] This is the thesis of Thom Hartmann's book, hence its title *The Last Hours of Ancient Sunlight*. [14] *Seeking the Kingdom*, pp. 15–16.

We will never get the forces of organized greed to yield to the needs of our dying planet until the very idea of destroying the planet affects us in the same way as murder, rape or terrorism. When the president of a big chemical company directs his subordinates to dump toxic wastes in the groundwater supply, and his employees react with the same horror as if he's told them to boil a young child alive, then the dumping will stop. This is a problem in moral awareness. And morality is the province of organized religion.[15]

One hopeful sign is how these issues are no longer simply the concerns of radical environmentalists but are more and more entering mainstream discussion. There is growing talk of 'peak oil' – that we have already passed the peak of oil and gas production and are in fact living at the end of what Thomas Berry calls 'the petroleum interval' in human history.[16] Today even the oil companies themselves predict increasing demand even as they are recording declining production.[17] The problem now is not so much raising awareness of the threats we face as offering wise leadership and modelling alternative ways of living and creating resilient communities to prepare ourselves for the radical changes that will be required of us.

At the Schumacher lectures in 2005, Jakob von Uexküll voiced an increasingly commonly-held view that probably the defining issue of our age is not only climate change but also our reactions to it (although since 2008 the state of the economy now occupies more media attention).[18] With atmospheric carbon levels estimated to be at their highest for the last 32 million years, with even a dim awareness of so much destruction (of the war against nature in which we are so often unconsciously implicated) how can we discover an effective response?

In my Swarthmore Lecture[19] I spoke of working with Joanna Macy and my experience of what she now calls 'the Work that Reconnects', the experiential practices which she has developed

15 'Uniting Friends with Nature', p. 29. 16 This is the title of chapter 13 of his book *The Great Work*. 17 See for instance 'Beyond Oil: the oil curse and solutions for an oil-free future', a pamphlet from Rising Tide, an Oxford-based action group on climate change, available on www.wrm.org.uy/deforestation/oil/BeyondOil.pdf 18 Opening address of the annual Schumacher lectures in Bristol in 2005 on the theme 'Shaping the Future'. 19 *A Faith to Call our Own* pp. 7–9.

with colleagues around the world over the past three decades. In some of the key exercises of this work, workshop participants assume the perspective of future generations, who, looking back to us as their ancestors, ask us questions such as 'What did you do that really made a difference?'; 'How did you get going in the face of what seemed impossible odds?'; 'How did you sustain yourselves when things looked bleak?'[20] This is a great example of what activist Chris Johnstone calls 'imaginary hindsight' and it feels essential to create spaces in which to imagine the way forward when the future is in question.

Joanna Macy describes the opportunity offered by the dangers we face: 'Like cells in a living body, we feel it when our larger body is in trauma … So how do we stand open-eyed in the face of apocalyptic events, and still find joy in serving life? And, if we can do that, what transformative powers will arise in us?'[21] We need to create safe places to explore these unfamiliar collective emotions, we need to create a culture in which we are not thought mad or 'over-sensitive' for being scared, angry, grief-struck or numb in the face of the global challenges we face. Precisely because these are far more than purely personal feelings (and not symptoms of a private neurosis) we need to create strong communities where we can safely explore and contain them. We simply can't deal with any of this alone; we can't even start to face the reality of our situation from a place of isolation. It feels overwhelming; we get stuck in despair (another understandable response where we need to be compassionate towards one another). It seems to me that faith communities – with their considerable human and physical resources, with their fine traditions of public forms of celebration, thanksgiving and lamentation – are an obvious place to start.

This is the real challenge today, to each ask ourselves what part we can play in this 'Great Turning', in the creation of a just and sustainable future for all beings. How do we respond to this essentially spiritual challenge? How do we personally align ourselves with this great work of our age? What resources can we bring, individually and collectively, in our faith communities to this task?

[20] *Coming Back to Life* pp. 135–148.

[21] Personal communication, but see www.joannamacy.net for similar reflections.

As Quakers we don't spend much time speculating on the Mystery that we wait upon in the stillness of worship; we don't speculate on 'the nature of God'. We have rejected credal assent, the agreement to propositions about the divine as the basis of our faith. Rather we have emphasised experiential knowing and we encourage one another to wait on and obey 'the promptings of love and truth' in our hearts. We try to respect the different ways we speak of our experience of divine Presence, knowing that the words we use are not what's really important. What we do agree about in our spiritual diversity is that in the act of stilling ourselves, of waiting expectantly, we can practise what Patricia Loring calls 'listening spirituality' in her book of that title. This listening/waiting/sensing is the basis for discerning action; we seek the guidance of the gathered meeting and from this place we may be led into service in 'the world'. In the silence/stillness of meeting or of private meditation and prayer we can be given a strong sense of what we must do to work for the realisation of 'the kingdom of heaven' here on Earth.

The essence of Quaker spirituality is our personal experience of and our collective witness to a sacred dimension of life that is greater than our limited human consciousness, a mystery at the heart of life which will guide us if we wait expectantly upon its leadings. As Friends we organise our lives to be responsive, to be faithful to the callings we are given in this way. I have a little postcard by my desk which reads: 'I am a Quaker: in case of emergency, please be quiet!'

The twentieth-century American Friend Douglas Steere said something crucial, I believe, when he observed that 'the true listener is vulnerable'. In his book *On Listening to Another*, he listed four qualities of a good listener; the first is vulnerability, followed by acceptance, expectancy, and constancy. I believe it is this quality of vulnerability, of humble 'listening' (actually sensing – with our bodies, our intuition and imagination, our human capacity to be sensitive to reality which goes far beyond hearing alone) – that Friends could bring to the spiritual crisis of our age.

Occasionally Friends have sensed something of this calling. In Yearly Meeting in session in 1988 we heard (and subsequently recorded in our minute) the words of the Zen monk and poet Thich Nhat Hanh: 'Now is the time to hear within us the sound of the Earth crying'.[22] And something of the same sense of anguished urgency, of radical realignment with Life on Earth could be heard in the vocal ministry of a young Friend at the residential Yearly Meeting at Exeter in 2001. A decade on from that, we are finding our collective voice; we seem to be moving towards articulating a Quaker testimony to the sacred integrity of the Earth. Our Canterbury Commitment, Minute 36 of Britain Yearly Meeting in 2011, may not be overtly couched in these terms, but this is certainly one valid reading of our new-found sense of corporate witness:

> A concern for the Earth and the well-being of all who dwell in it is not new, and we have not now received new information which calls us to act. Rather we are renewing our commitment to a sense of the unity of creation which has always been part of Friends' testimonies.[23]

What would it mean to really be open to 'the sounds of the Earth' within us; to make our business decisions in the firm belief that we are a part of, not apart from, the rest of life; that our choices now inevitably impact on generations yet unborn? What would it mean to allow for the possibility that ancestors and those not yet graced with life might want to be given voice in meeting for worship? What if we really took on board the words of spiritual teacher Alan Watts: 'You didn't come into this world. You came out of it, like a wave from the ocean. You are not a stranger here'.[24]

In the expectant waiting of Quaker worship those present have the expectation to be put in touch with a sense of wonder at the awesome generosity of life, the mystery at the heart of all existence. What Friends collectively have to offer (what we have to offer) in this time is our three hundred and sixty year experience of trusting our encounter with what Thomas Kelly calls an 'objective, dynamic Presence', and a 'super-individual Life and Power'.[25] The real challenge for us as Western, industrialised human beings, is to also 'hear' (be sensitive to) this Presence

[22] Thich Nhat Hanh quoted in Macy & Brown, *Coming Back to Life*, p. 91. [23] Britain Yearly Meeting 2011 Minute 36, *Our Canterbury Commitment*. [24] Quoted in Macy, *Despair and Personal Power in the Nuclear Age*, p. 31. [25] *The Gathered Meeting*, p. 53.

within the more-than-human world. Susannah Kay Brindle, an Australian Friend much influenced by her respectful contact with aboriginal Australians, expresses this sensibility when she writes:

> There is a longing in the Earth itself and among indigenous peoples everywhere for us to awaken and come home to the reality of the Spirit in the More-than-Human world. There is a need for us to share our experiences, to become clear about what we believe and about the ways in which those beliefs oblige us to act. Perhaps, then, in our prayers, in our worship, in our Quaker action, we may at last be ready to listen to the voices of the Earth and 'to learn a new song'.[26]

In speaking to diverse audiences around the world, the visionary author and educator Duane Elgin (who describes himself as 'an evolutionary activist'), asks his listeners this question: 'When you look at human behaviour around the world and then imagine our species as an individual, how old would that person be?' All over the world, within seconds the majority of his audience have responded the same way: at least two thirds say that humanity is in its teenage years. Teenagers, especially male ones, are reckless, they act without regard for the consequences of their actions; they believe, in a sense that they are 'immortal'. Former U.S. vice-president Al Gore, in his book *Earth in the Balance* wrote: '... a civilisation that has, like an adolescent, acquired new powers but not the maturity to use them wisely also runs the risk of an unrealistic sense of immortality and a dulled perception of serious danger'.[27]

What we are facing is our necessary 'coming of age', our potential initiation into adulthood as a species. Thomas Berry talks in many of his books and articles of what is needed in this time as nothing less than 'the reinvention of the human at the species level'[28] – which will mean discovering a genuine humility, an awareness of the greater whole of which we are a part. Theologically this is a time when increasing numbers of us feel called to recognise that there is not, finally, some cosmic super-parent to pick up after us and rescue us from our responsibilities.

[26] *To Learn a New Song*, p. 50. [27] *Earth in the Balance*, p. 213
[28] See John Grims' biographical essay: 'Time, History, Historians in Thomas Berry's Vision', http://Thomasberry.org/Biography

Seen in the context of our 'coming of age', an evolving sense of the divine – the 'death of God', the movement away from a theistic God as a rescuing (or judging) super-parental 'Other' – can actually be seen not as a loss of faith but as a maturing. Our changing imagining of the divine is an aspect of growing up, of seeking our true human responsibility, our particular role in the unfolding cosmic drama. Jesus' image of God as father then becomes not the basis of a dogmatic, Trinitarian theology maintained by church doctrine, but merely an accurate expression of our intimacy and true dependence upon the mystery at the heart of the universe-event.

Duane Elgin sees humanity in just this way, engaged collectively in a crucial rite of passage. 'Humanity', he predicts, 'is about to move into a stage of initiation – a period of stress and testing in which we will be challenged to discover ourselves as a single family with responsibilities to one another, the Earth, and future generations'.[29]

Anthropologists point out that in other cultures there are rites of passage that formalise the process of accepting the rights and responsibilities of adulthood – and that these come at the point where we need to internalise the reality of personal death. Joanna Macy sees that on our planetary journey, humanity has perhaps reached a similar stage. For the first time in our history 'we perceive the possibility of the death of our species'. In which case, 'facing our despair and anguish for our world is, in effect, a kind of initiatory rite, necessary to our growing up, required for our maturation as a species'.[30]

I would argue that this acceptance of our present condition is not morbid, something to be avoided. Working among Quakers I find it hard when people insist we should be positive – rather than letting hope and creativity emerge because we have dared to face our fears, our grief, even our despair. True hope arises, in my experience, from a different place – from something built into the fabric of our world. Hope, as the playwright and first president of the Czech republic Vaclav Havel put it, is 'an orientation of the spirit, an orientation of the heart', transcending the world of immediate experience;

[29] *Promise Ahead*, p. 8. [30] Letter, September 7, 2005 http://joannamacy.net/joannasletters/145-september72005.html

'Hope is not the same as joy that things are going well ... but rather, an ability to work for something because it is good'.[31] Hope in this deep sense is ultimately the ground of everything we attempt to do; it is the expression of our faith, our ultimately unverifiable trust in the integrity and meaningfulness of life's unfolding. Standing on this Earth, we are given not certainty that we will succeed but the capacity for choice, the extraordinary evolutionary gift of human intention. Without any guarantees, we can choose to commit ourselves to life's continuation. The Australian rain-forest activist John Seed said: 'I want my life to be a vote against extinction.'[32]

What these challenging times demand of us is, first and foremost, a quality of presence, a mature sense not of controlling and managing the world, but a profound sense of being in attendance, present and able to respond. Joanna Macy sees the similarities in attending a birth and being with someone who is dying. In both situations, she says, 'we can only be grateful for this moment, this breath, this incredible capacity to direct our attention'. The potential of where we find ourselves today is that this could be 'a moment of unparalleled awakening'. She combines an extraordinary love of life with a dispassionate ability to simply see what is before her:

I don't think we've been given any absolute guarantee that conscious life on Earth will continue. It might. It might not. In either case, this is a most extraordinary and beautiful moment. Because in this moment we can make a choice for loving life and taking care of each other. Right up to the end, we can make that choice, and that's glorious. So we don't need to ask, 'Will it go on forever?' This moment is forever. In this moment I can honour the ancestors, honour the future beings, honour you, and the beautiful work we are all doing. And there's no end to that.[33]

From the great religious traditions we have examples of what it means for individuals to awaken, to become enlightened to their true nature. But the evolutionary pressure that is on us now

[31] *Disturbing the Peace*, p. 181. [32] Personal communication to Chris Johnstone, campaigner and then editor of The Great Turning Times email newsletter www.greatturningtimes.org [33] Letter, September 7, 2005 http://joannamacy.net/nasletters/145-september72005.html

calls for nothing less than a collective awakening. We can scarcely imagine what that will entail. But as we remember our long evolutionary journey we can take some comfort from those times in the past when the future of life on Earth must have seemed just as uncertain as it does today. The difference is that we are creatures who are aware of the destruction and our responsibility for it. Just as the awareness of death for an individual engenders an appreciation of the sacred mystery of life, so too our collective awakening may be precipitated by nothing less than the threat of extinction.

Chapter 4
Coming Down to Earth

Jo Farrow

Without the wild world we are less than we could be: less than ourselves.

Simon Barnes[1]

What do I make of all this texture? What does it mean about the kind of world in which I have been set down? The texture of the world, its filigree and scrollwork, it means that there is the possibility of beauty here, a beauty inexhaustible in its complexity, which opens to my knock, which answers to me a call I do not remember calling, and which trains me to the wild and extravagant nature of the spirit I seek.

Annie Dillard[2]

I was three years old when I had my first experience of the numinous or what someone has called 'The Big Holy' or 'The Great Holy'. Or, if you like it was my first awareness that I was related to everything in the universe and everything in it was somehow connected to everything else. And I knew that the whole thing was very mysterious and wonderful.

I was on holiday in East Sussex with my grandparents. I had been taken by my mother and grandfather on a walk to the local recreation ground. A square of it was kept very nice and neat for cricket matches and football. The rest was wild and much more interesting to me. While they sat on a bench against the wall of

[1] *Birds* (Royal Society for the Protection of Birds magazine), May 2007, p. 23. [2] *Pilgrim at Tinker Creek*, p. 127

the cricket pavilion and talked together I wandered away from the nice, neat bit. (And I've been doing that ever since!) I wandered into the long grass round the edge of the pitch. In places the grass was very high, taller than I was. The sun shone through it making it luminous and full of wonder to me.

I have no idea how long I stood there or how long I wandered in that field of bright grasses. I only know that I was aware of being alive in a world full of greenness and light and colour and it was marvellous. I loved it passionately. It was so beautiful, and so full of movement and mystery that something in me was crying 'Yes' to it all. I was blown out of my infant mind into that place where there is no beginning or ending of anything, where everything in the universe is connected to everything else. I knew that I was a part of it all, bonded to the earth and the sun, to the sky, to every flower and every blade of grass. It was my first remembered experience of knowing, inwardly and deeply, what the universe is really like.

It was over thirty years before I was able to call back that memory, and bring into my consciousness that moment of wonder and deep knowing in a field of bright grasses. In 1964, (as I have described it in Chapter 1) I was in one of those transitional periods when you know that one way of life has ended for you and you are, like Abraham, going out into the unknown. It's an exciting but terrifying time because you don't know what will be left when you finally let go of the old way and take a step towards the new.

The old way that ended for me, at that moment in 1964, was being a 'professional religious' and working in an almost totally church-centred world. During those 12 years I had gained lots of things – a passion for theology, time for study and reflection, recognition of my personal priesthood, a ministry to which I knew I was called. But I had lost some things that were equally important to me. I had certainly moved further and further away from the deep knowing of those moments in a field of bright grasses, as I suppose we all move away from the vivid intuitions of early childhood.

In the Deaconess College I read theology under the shadow of Karl Barth, the great Swiss theologian. He was a fierce opponent of what was then called 'Natural Theology'. He was sure that Nature could tell us nothing about God. All that we can know about God, he argued, comes by way of revelation, by which he meant the Scriptures or some special religious experience of encounter with God. At three years old I was a better theologian than that. I knew that the whole earth is a revelation. Revelation was shining and shimmering through those luminous grasses, telling me that I was part of a cosmos in which everything was sacred, everything related to everything else and that just to be in such a universe was a communion experience. Of course I could not have put it into those words at that time.

When I began my training as a deaconess, over fifty years ago, it was a celibate order that I was entering. I have always been surprised that a Protestant women's deaconate in the Free Church tradition should, at that time, have taken on board all the dualisms and hierarchies of the ecclesiastic mediaeval mindset, but it had. It was crammed with all the world-renouncing, body-rejecting negativities of classical Christian Platonism. I wanted, at that time, more than anything else, to be a woman of God, a holy woman and if that meant saying 'No' to any number of pleasurable and satisfying experiences I was willing to accept those renunciations. I was such a spiritual toddler that I had no idea how destructive that version of Christian holiness could be.

The most damaging thing about it was the view of the world and nature that was assumed throughout our theological training. It was not simply the Barthian view that nature can tell us nothing about God. The main assumptions, as Joanna Macy observes in her *World as Lover, World as Self*, were that the world was either a battleground where good and evil waged their unceasing war, or a distraction from the main task of holiness.[3]

In Protestant terms the underlying message was that of Bunyan's *Pilgrim's Progress*, that the world is a wilderness, bleak and unsatisfactory, though full of tempting distractions and traps for the unwary. The job of the Christian, therefore was to turn his or her face away from this world and begin a journey to a more enduring and satisfactory place. I suspect that Bunyan's spiritual classic, and scores of books of devotion and piety based on its assumptions, have conditioned many of us in spite of our Quaker

[3] *World as Lover, World as Self*, p. 5–7

affirmations about the goodness of creation and the sacramental nature of the whole of life.

I adopted a way of life sustained by a wealth of devotional literature and pious exercises inspired by that Platonist/Calvinistic version of Christian faith. I knew next to nothing about church history at that point and I had no idea that I was buying into a spiritual tradition modelled on monasticism and therefore designed by celibate men, most of whom were haunted by Plato's ghost, and his obsession with other-worldly perfection. Nor did I realise that it was a system which would effectively condition me to betray my own experiences, the things I knew most deeply.

Two of the most pervasive images of the spiritual life that have dominated male expressions of spirituality are 'the ladder of ascent' and that of 'the journey'. Both images assume that there is a destination to be reached and that it can only be reached after arduous effort, generally a lifetime of effort. Indeed the main thrust of much traditional spirituality has been the idea of going from where you are, which is seen as unsatisfactory, to some idealised place where the awkward, depressing, changeful aspects of this life have all been eradicated.

Women writers on spirituality have begun to question these metaphors of the spiritual life. Carol Ochs, in *Women and Spirituality*, argues that the image of journeying is not helpful because it suggests 'that part of our life has value only insofar as it contributes to achieving the destination'.[4] Instead of the 'journey' metaphor Carol Ochs proposes 'the spiritual walk' as a possible alternative. It may not have the same appeal as the journey motif but it has the advantage of being down-to-earth. A walk, she argues, doesn't have to have a clear destination. It doesn't necessarily have to go anywhere. It can be long or short and enjoyed for its own sake. Our eyes are not fixed on some distant horizon and therefore we can notice all the things around us and enjoy them. The walk is about 'being in the here-and-now', and finding the sacred always in the process of life itself, in the present, rather than the future tense.

Matthew Fox observes that there is no theme in all of male dominated mystical teaching in Western Christianity that is more recurrent than that of climbing Jacob's Ladder. He cites

[4] *Women and Spirituality*, p. 118

the fact that in the *Dictionnaire de Spiritualité*, an encyclopaedia of numerous volumes dedicated to Western Spirituality, the entry under 'spiritual ladder' comprises twenty-four full columns and includes an apology from the author because his treatment of the subject has been 'only partial'.[5]

In the beginning of the Christian story many of those who joined the Christian community were slaves or, as Paul observed, 'not many mighty, not many noble'. God, he suggested, had chosen the weak and those who were marginalised to put to shame the powerful and influential.[6] The way of Christian spirituality was open to all whatever their rank or social class. But eventually all that changed, and the spiritual life became something so rarefied and elitist that only those in religious orders who had turned their backs on the world could hope to rise very far in it, rise being the operative word.

Ladder Spirituality was all about rising, climbing away from earthly things and refusing to be distracted by the world. It was based, oddly enough, on a folk story in the Old Testament, the story of Jacob and his dream. Jacob was a wheeler-dealer of the first order. At the beginning of his story he emerges as a liar, a thief and a cheat. He cheats his brother out of his rightful inheritance and has to make a quick getaway before his brother finds out. In his flight he is forced to sleep rough in the desert. While he is asleep he has one of those really vivid dreams that are still with you when you wake up. He dreams that there is a ladder erected between the place where he is sleeping and heaven, and on the ladder there are angels, messengers of God, going up and down between earth and heaven. He is so shaken by his dream that he says, 'Surely God was right here, and I didn't realise it', and he makes a kind of altar because he says 'this is a holy place, the gate of heaven, the house of God'.[7] His response is to name earth as the holy ground and the place where God is found.

One of the really astonishing things in the story of Christian spirituality is how that 'down to earth' vision of the two-way traffic between human beings and God, even between God and shady opportunists like Jacob, became totally reversed. A type of spirituality emerged in the sixth century, which was based on Jacob's Ladder, but which turned the whole thing upside down. Instead

---

5 *A Spirituality Named Compassion*, p. 37

6 1 Corinthians 1:27–28.   7 Genesis 28:16–17

of a continual commerce between heaven and earth, bringing blessings to good and bad alike, the ladder became a one-way passage, a steep and hazardous ladder of ascent to a God who was remote and inaccessible to all but a few intrepid climbers.

Margaret Miles refers to a vivid icon of the 'Ladder of Ascent' in the front of a book by St. John Climacus.[8] It shows a number of monks climbing the ladder. All the way up there are demons trying to pull them off. At the top there are one or two very superior ecclesiastic persons in the dress of Abbots or Archbishops, being welcomed into heaven. There are no lay people on the ladder, and no women or children. Manuals about climbing the Ladder of Ascent were written for ordinary lay people but it was assumed that they would have great difficulty in climbing it and getting as far up as those who were full-time 'religious' giving their whole lives to prayer and devotional reading, to fasting and other pietistic and ascetic exercises.

It is, alas, a vivid picture of what happened to Christian spirituality. It became concentrated, not on earth or this world, not on the goodness of creation, but on heaven and the next world. The further away from earthly things you climbed the nearer you would get to heaven. In fact, everything to do with earth and 'earthiness', bodies and human sexuality, and women, of course, was distracting, and a snare and delusion to pull you off the ladder and down to earth again, or even lower. Some pictures of the Ladder of Ascent showed those who fell off toppling downwards into the horrifying torments of hell. The model of Ladder Spirituality was basically about the renunciation of earthly things. It began the long process of creating spiritual hierarchies and dualisms – sacred versus secular, spiritual versus material, spirit versus flesh, soul versus body, men versus women, here versus there, and so on.

Whether we are aware of it or not most of us have been to some extent conditioned by some of the ideas behind Ladder Spirituality, or what came to be known as the 'Ladder of Ascent' or the 'Ladder of Perfection'. I managed to do it in a rather dramatic way by becoming one of those full-time 'religious', and although it was a women's order in the Protestant/Free Church tradition it was certainly contaminated by the fall-out from many

8 *The Image and Practice of Holiness*, p. 66.

of the most damaging aspects of Ladder Spirituality. It was an order with a vow of lifelong commitment. We went where we were sent without choice or question. It discouraged close relations of any kind as being distractions from the path of holiness. Spirituality was about a disciplined practice of prayer, devotional reading, Bible study, good works and service. The aim, of course, was not enjoyment of life, but an uphill struggle in which doing really difficult things for God earned you spiritual Brownie points and got you further up the Ladder of Perfection.

The Platonist version of Christian faith is still seductive, of course, otherwise it would not have been so invasive and persistent. It was particularly seductive in those long centuries when for most people life was nasty, brutish and short, when there were no labour-saving devices and no anaesthetics. It is still seductive to those who can't bear the uncertainties, contradictions and messiness of human life and who long to rise above it. Transcending the ordinary unpredictability of things for something more rarefied appeals to quite a lot of people, and even some New Age versions of spirituality have fallen into it. The Platonic version was grafted onto the Jesus revolution so swiftly and effectively that it was hardly apparent, except to a few, that the human, down-to-earth and life-loving religion of a charismatic Jewish prophet had been transmuted into its opposite.

When I began to be aware of how much I had allowed myself to be diminished by that system and realised that for me that particular way of life was coming to an end, I took an unpaid sabbatical year in order to think, pray and reflect on what the next part of my spiritual journey might be. Two possibilities were emerging. I had had a number of articles published in various journals and 20 poems published in an anthology of new verse. I wondered whether I was being led into some kind of writing ministry, but another part of me, buried for years under an avalanche of Barthian theology and other-worldly piety, was my delight in colour and visual imagery and my love of painting. I was more and more drawn to that and wondered whether my new ministry might be in art therapy. Eventually the need to be creative with visual images began to emerge as the more important thing for me at that point.

In order to persuade an art college to accept a middle-aged deaconess as a student I had to paint as much as I could. During that time I met Marian Milner, a Jungian analyst and art therapist. She invited me to one of her art therapy sessions and introduced me to the practice of painting from the unconscious, simply allowing forms and patterns, and colour to emerge in response to a kind of inner listening. That was when I recovered my memory of being in that field of bright grasses. I went home and began a series of paintings of a shining pathway between tall grasses. I knew that it was a memory of something important that had happened to me, but I still wasn't sure what it was. I remembered that I had also recently written a series of poems about grass. Then I came across Edith Sitwell's 'How many Heavens', with its marvellous first line 'The emeralds are singing in the grasses'[9] and, suddenly, I was back in that bright field again, remembering.

I had never been completely at ease with the more traditional symbols of the Easter story and orthodox assumptions that it is historical fact rather than profound myth, but I realised that grass had always been a symbol for me of new life, of resurrection. Whenever I walked across the Yorkshire moors or the Sussex downs a swathe of green grasses moving like an inland sea would start a kind of singing inside me, doxologies and glorias and Easter-like carolling. 'Now the green blade riseth' was one of the few Easter carols that really spoke to me, and I suppose that too was a reminder of my first experience of a revelatory universe and my intimate connection with the earth itself.

As I've suggested, the theology that had conditioned my religious life was that of the Judeo-Christian tradition and the Protestant-Calvinist emphasis on the Bible, sin and depravity, and the need for redemption. Yet even when I was being trained as a deaconess, reading theology and being soaked in the Fall/Atonement version, I realised that my natural way of responding to the holy (which was creation-centred long before Matthew Fox wrote *Original Blessing*), was not regarded as 'kosher' at all. Then, as now, my most vivid awareness of the holy came to me not in the places or times that orthodox Christians labelled sacred, but out on the moors in Yorkshire, where the Deaconess College was at

[9] *Collected Poems*, p. 306.

that time, or on the Sussex downs where I grew up, and later in flower-hunting forays in high Alpine meadows.

It wasn't surprising then, that for much longer than I care to remember I felt that I was odd and out of step. I felt guilty that traditional ways of prayer and worship meant so much less to me than being in wild and remote places, walking in woods or on the sea shore, or across the moors. I felt uneasy that I was much more inwardly refreshed by these things, or by sharing a meal with friends, listening to music, reading a stimulating book, painting a picture or flower-hunting in the Alps, than by any of the devotional exercises that were supposed to nourish me spiritually.

For years, only two writers from the tradition of Christian spirituality gave me any hope that my delight in the natural world and my experiences of the holy within it were a valid part of the Christian tradition. One was Thomas Traherne, a contemporary of George Fox and one of the few Christian mystics with a passionate, exuberant delight in the natural world. The other was the Jesuit priest and palaeontologist, Teilhard de Chardin, who struggled throughout his life to reconcile his sense of a revelatory universe with the Catholic theology he was supposed to teach. In the end the Church forbade him to teach or to publish any of his work. In his 'Mass on the World' he sees the world as the Body of God.[10] Nearly seventy years later, feminist theologian Sallie McFague wrote two books on the theme of the world as God's body. 'The world is our meeting place with God' she wrote '... as the body of God it is wondrously, awesomely, divinely mysterious'.[11]

Today there are many women articulating an earth-loving spirituality and affirming that a sense of deep connection with the earth is an important part of their religious awareness. Nowadays religious bookshops have shelves crammed with books on Celtic spirituality with its celebration of the whole of creation, books on Green spirituality, Native American spirituality, and, of course, the work of people like Thomas Berry and Brian Swimme and Matthew Fox. But that time was still to come. In 1964 there were few books on the themes of creation spirituality and the only major book on the ecological crisis was Rachel

---

10 *Hymn of the Universe*, pp. 36–37. 11 *Models of God*, p. 69

Carson's *Silent Spring*. Even in those long ago days I was still very much a 'believer in exile'.

At the end of my sabbatical year I had managed to persuade Leeds College of Art that my work showed sufficient promise for me to be enrolled for a four-year degree course. They were rather sceptical about whether a middle-aged deaconess, moving out of the narrowness of a church-centred world would be able to cope with the kind of radical change involved in becoming an art student in the 'swinging sixties'. The head of the Art Department continued to look doubtfully at me and expressed his apprehension on more than one occasion, until I appeared in one of his seminars smoking a bright magenta pipe! Sometimes you have to take desperate measures to break out of someone else's stereotyping. It was the first and last time I ever smoked a pipe.

That was the beginning of the end of my struggle to fit myself into the milieu of traditional Christianity, although it was actually another fourteen years before I finally left the deaconess order and began to attend a Quaker meeting. I never returned to that narrow church-centred world. Instead I taught Art and Design, first as a research fellow in what was then Leeds Polytechnic and later in a school for children with serious learning difficulties. Halfway through my two year stint as a research fellow, my partner got a job in University College, Cardiff. I travelled from Leeds to Cardiff every weekend until my fellowship came to an end and I managed to get a place in a postgraduate teaching course in Cardiff.

It was during that difficult time of commuting from north to west that I had another overwhelming 'peak' experience or 'Opening'. I had travelled down from Leeds to Cardiff late on Friday night. I was tired and depressed about my research, which wasn't going very well. On Saturday we got a bus to Llantwit Major and spent the day ambling along the cliffs. I didn't realise at the time that Llantwit was one of the main sites of Celtic Christianity, and perhaps its creation-centred ambience, embedded in rock and stone along that coast, had something to do with what happened. It was a glorious day in a Spring that had been late in arriving. The sun shone on an incredibly blue sea. Great clumps of thrift bloomed along the edge of the cliffs. We came on a field of cowslips glowing gold and glistening in the spring sunlight. And then, almost immediately we came to a narrow valley blazing with the rich crimson-purple of early purple orchids. I remember that a green woodpecker flew out from under the cliffs and away to a small wood. The wood shone with that incredible fresh green of spring foliage. Suddenly, and for the rest of that day I was like George Fox, back in Eden, with 'the creation opened to me'.[12] I was completely at one with everything, with no sense of simply observing the world, but aware instead of being an intimate part of it all.

The trouble is, of course, that there are no words with which to express those deep, deep experiences of unity with creation. It was what C.S. Lewis called 'A Day with a White Mark'.[13] Though perhaps 'white' is not the adjective. Hildegard of Bingen comes closer to it when she coined the word 'viriditas' to express the living greenness of a world which is always pulsing with life and wonder. So perhaps I should call it my 'Day with a Green Mark'.

In spite of these experiences, in spite of my sense of deep affinity with the natural world, I still had moments of struggling to reconcile this with the theological emphases of mainstream Christianity. Every religious broadcast or TV programme was dominated by those church-centred Fall and Atonement theologies, as they still are. I was still uneasy because I was so out of step with orthodox Christian spirituality. I think I have been a very slow learner for I found it desperately difficult to free myself from the negative aspects of that kind of theology, but perhaps I am not alone in this. Two thousand years of Christian art and poetry, in addition to church dogma and ritual, have hammered home the Fall/Atonement view of spirituality. There were poets, of course, who wrote of a different view of the world and one that was very much creation-centred, poets like Kathleen Raine, whose 'Northumbrian Sequence'[14] expressed some of the things of which I had been aware in those 'peak' experiences of oneness with creation.

When I came among Friends it was easier in some ways. The silence offered a space to reflect and dive deep, to explore inner space, to listen to what was really happening on the inside of

[12] *Journal*, ed. Nickalls, p. 27, (entry for 1648). [13] *The Poems of C.S. Lewis*, p. 28. [14] *Collected Poems*, p. 111.

my life. I no longer had to listen to hymns or sermons that were alien to me. These were all good and liberating things. But the language of Quaker spirituality in its foundation stories was still 'religious language' which ranked spirit above body, sacrificial obedience above delight in the blessings of creation. In fact the language of George Fox in his sermons was somehow less compassionate and far more judgemental than the language of Jesus in the Synoptic Gospels. Indeed the ethos of Quaker spirituality was more a heavy obligation to mend the world than to relish its wonder and beauty, or at any rate, with no sense that both occupations were equally important. Only the Quaker plant hunters and botanists balanced for me the early Quaker obsession with costly obedience and perfection.

When I learned of my appointment as General Secretary of what was then Quaker Home Service, I booked myself in for one of the '1652 Country' pilgrimages. I thought this would be a good preparation for the work I would have to do in Friends House. One of the things we did, of course, was to toil up Pendle Hill in the footsteps of George Fox. Needless to say he went up by the steepest route. There is a relatively easy way of going up but the hang-over from the world-rejecting version of Christianity says that you must always do things the hard way!

It's possible that I am one of the few Friends who has never managed to get to the top of Pendle Hill. The group I was with set off at a cracking pace. And I was soon left behind. Only one Friend, about the same age as me, kept me company. Then she too went on ahead of me, and I was left alone on that fell side with only the sound of the wind, and water falling over rocks, the faint bleating of lambs and the plaintive crying of curlews.

The rest of our party made it to the top of Pendle. I had my satori on the lower slopes. And I learned at least three things that were important to me. I learned that I had no desire to go back to the past for my models of holiness. I knew, in any case, that what George Fox discovered was not something accessible to me simply because I was treading in his footsteps, and that his vision of the world was not mine and never could be. Over 300 years of rigorous biblical scholarship lay between us, to say nothing of mind-blowing discoveries about the universe in which we live. My world is post-Freudian, post-Marxist, post Einstein and quantum physics, post Holocaust, post the women's movement, and post the discovery of anaesthetics and genetic engineering. There was no way in which our visions could be the same.

Secondly, I found that I was at home on that wild fell side. Something in that remote place spoke to a wildness in me, belonging perhaps to that time before the human species came out of the wilderness and domesticated their animals and themselves. A Mexican Jungian psychoanalyst, Clarissa Pinkola Estes, has written a strange and powerful book called *Women who Run with the Wolves*. It's a book written to encourage women to reclaim the wild places in themselves, which are places of power and creative energy. I think that what I discovered on the slopes of Pendle Hill was that the something in me which responds to the elemental wildness of a northern fell is also the part of me that responds to the wild calling of the Spirit. After all, the symbols with which the first friends of Jesus described the eruption of the Spirit into their lives were the elemental ones of wind and fire. And the Celtic symbol of the Holy Spirit is not the dove but the wild goose. I discovered once again my own lost vision of a creation-centred spirituality.

Thirdly, I learned that my spirituality was not about transcending the world in order to go in quest of the ideal. It was an earthy kind of spirituality, creation-centred, recognising the here-and-now, the place where I am, as the 'Holy Ground'. My spirituality would always be, whether it was offbeat or frowned on by orthodox Christians, or even orthodox Quakers, a spirituality rooted in the earth, a spirituality which sees glory in the ordinary, and in the extraordinary wonder of creation itself, which finds the universe itself the primary place of revelation.

Looking back at the event now I can see something else that I didn't see at the time. From childhood I had received messages from a perfectionist mother, and then, later, from a church that insisted on the striving for perfection. And, as a rule, I would have sweated up that hillside and refused to give in. That was the kind of spirituality I had inherited – 'if it doesn't hurt it isn't working', or what Lavinia Byrne calls the 'cling to the rock and bleed' version of discipleship, what early Quakers called the 'the

Test of the Cross', the 'No Cross, No Crown' version of Quakerism. And, as Lavinia Byrne suggests, 'This forms a terrible trav-
esty of the great call at the heart of Christian living, the call to
love ... The lives of the saints are littered with stories of people
who had alarming ideas about how best to please God, women
and men who went for the hard option'.[15] I find that among
Friends there is a tendency to revere the kind of spirituality that
goes for the hard option.

When I finally came to work in Friends House I relished
being able to browse in the bookshop and I discovered all the
books that ended my sense of spiritual isolation. There were
books which introduced me to what women were writing about
their spirituality. And for most of them it was definitely an earth-
centred spirituality. It was in the bookshop too that I first discovered Matthew Fox and his passionate commitment to the
lost tradition of creation-centred spirituality. With those two discoveries – the spirituality that women were reclaiming, and the
creation spirituality that Mathew Fox was busy re-discovering, my
long sense of being spiritually out of step came to an end.

I found that it still wasn't easy to disentangle myself from
the dominant assumptions of the mainstream Christian tradition. They seemed to go on clinging to me like so many starving
ticks. Nor were some Friends very sympathetic to my enthusiasm
for Matthew Fox or my attempts to talk about a creation-centred
spirituality. One Friend in our Monthly Meeting said 'I find what
you say compelling but very frightening. It unsettles me.' A Jewish Friend, who had been in Nazi Germany on Kristallnacht felt
that I was ignoring the dark and threatening aspects of life. I
knew this was not true. For if you really become sensitised to the
awesome wonder of the natural world and know yourself an intimate part of it, you also become sensitised to the cry of the hungry, the marginalised and oppressed, to the crying of the earth,
the pain of our polluted and plundered planet.

Phyllis Windle, botanist, professional environmentalist and
also a hospital chaplain, writes about her grief at the reported
death of dogwood trees in America. As a hospital chaplain she
was aware that almost all the literature on grief and bereavement

[15] *Women Before God*, p. 62

related to the death of humans. To her surprise she became aware that the descriptions of mourning recounted in bereavement literature corresponded to the way in which she experienced the death of those trees.[16]

I remembered how in the hurricane of 1987, when eight million trees were destroyed across the south of England I nearly went mad with grief. We live next door to a cemetery and when I went out at first light most of the trees were broken off and lying on the ground and the whole scene was like a Paul Nash painting of a First World War battlefield. It felt as if something vital in me was broken too. For months after that event I went through the processes of grieving that we associate with the loss of someone very close to us. I felt something of this too during the foot and mouth crisis, when the human agenda and the profit motive were considered the priorities, and thousands upon thousands of animals were slaughtered (some researchers say quite needlessly), and treated with a barbarity that was not far removed from the gas chambers of Auschwitz.

Some years ago a Friend sent me *Easter Mysteries*, tape recordings of Matthew Fox's two talks at Findhorn in 1991 during the Easter weekend. In them he speaks on a theme which recurs in his work and forms the basis of his book, *The Coming of the Cosmic Christ*. Its theme is the Christian Passion or Paschal story, but in it he speaks of the contemporary Passion story as the dying of the earth. It is the earth that is being crucified, destroyed by the same destructive forces that brought about the death of Jesus. It is the earth as the body of God, which is being done to death by our addictive societies.

Thomas Berry's book *The Dream of the Earth* was the best antidote to my Barthian theology that I can imagine. Berry was convinced that we are at one of the most significant moments of grace and crisis that the human race has ever faced. The old creation story, that is, the Biblical creation story, which gave rise to the Atonement/Fall theologies in the Christian tradition no longer speaks to us with power. It does not really help us to make sense of where we are now. We know now that we are not children of a world that was created complete and perfect and then

16 'The Ecology of Grief', in *Ecopsychology*, pp. 137–138

contaminated by human arrogance and disobedience. We know that we are the products of an evolutionary universe, vast beyond our imagining, which is still in the process of evolving, developing, creating.

When I responded to an invitation from New Zealand Yearly Meeting and travelled there from the United States, I had not had a chance to read *The Dream of the Earth*. I discovered it in the bookshop at Pendle Hill Quaker Center for Study and Contemplation near Philadelphia, and it was part of a large parcel of books which had been despatched to Sussex for me to relish on my return. But I learned experientially the truth of what Thomas Berry was saying. My first Quaker engagement was to speak at a women's conference on Waiheki Island. I was expecting to give a talk about women's spirituality and that was all. To my consternation I discovered that I was expected to lead the whole weekend. I prefer to prepare very thoroughly for any engagement of this kind and there I was, with just one carefully prepared talk – and nothing else. In addition to this I was, in fact, ill and completely exhausted.

Waiheki Island is very beautiful and the Quaker conference centre is perched on a hill just above the north shore. In sheer desperation I knew that I had to trust the group itself and the island on which we were staying to be our resources for the weekend. So I sent every one off on a meditation walk, on their own, to bring back anything they found in their walk that spoke to them of the holy. I wish now that I had tape-recorded what happened when the women came back from their walk. For I can't remember a half of what was said. I only remember that as each woman laid down her shell or stone, seaweed or piece of driftwood or whatever had spoken to her, it was incredibly moving to hear what she said about it and why it symbolised for her the sacredness of the earth. But that is, in fact, what happened. The desacralising influence of the technocratic, consumer societies of which we were all a part was suddenly loosened and the earth itself was once again sacred and the place of revelation to us.

I found that the same thing happened at the Easter Gathering at the Friends settlement at Wanganui in the North Island. By this time I had travelled to the South Island, run a series of workshops, developed candida and been provisionally diagnosed as diabetic. I was, after a month of workshops and conferences, very tired and longing to go home. But again the weather was kind to us for the first part of the weekend and Easter Saturday was a warm, mellow autumn day. Again I suggested a meditation walk. This time I asked Friends to find something in their walk that spoke to them of the sacred and of the Easter story, to bring back whatever resonated for them and to write a poem or paint something to symbolise why it had special significance for them.

We met in a large room, which I think was an art room, and on a very large sheet of paper Friends put their found objects. Some painted something that symbolised their sense of the holy. Others wrote poems or put their reflections into prose. Then we stood together round the table looking at what we had done and holding hands. Some Friends spoke about what they had found. To my astonishment one Friend wrote to my meeting in Littlehampton to thank them for my ministry among them. In her letter she said that what we had done together had made the meaning of the Easter story come alive for her. But again it was the earth that had been our teacher, the real place of learning for us, and one of the things that had emerged loud and clear in the poems and writing was a sense of the interrelatedness of everything, and of the natural world as our place of meeting with God.

I learned still more about what it means to have a spiritual discipline that is creation-centred, and allows the universe itself to be our teacher, when I responded to the invitation of a local Catholic priest to attend a series of video lectures given by Brian Swimme, a mathematical physicist, and a close associate of Matthew Fox and Thomas Berry. The series was called *Canticle to the Cosmos*. They were, without a doubt, the most mind-blowing lectures I have ever seen and heard. My own background is in the arts and theology; I am a novice where science is concerned – which may be why I found the lectures a shattering experience.

Brian Swimme is a deeply spiritual person, a scientist who is also a mystic. He is a man with a passion to help people understand that the universe is revelatory and that a spirituality grounded on its basic characteristics will be one that honours the sacred in every other being, one that understands, with heart as well as mind, the interrelatedness of everything in the universe, and one that experiences the earth as sacred space, rather than real estate and a target for human exploitation.

He is quite clear about what this means for us as human beings and some of what he says is salutary for us as Quakers. If you want to know and co-operate in the adventure of the universe and what it will do next in terms of its creativity, he says, 'Follow what allures you. What really attracts you.' This is a very difficult discipline for good people, he suggests, because good people can go on doing for year after year things that actually bore them!

I was so impressed by the *Canticle to the Cosmos* that I decided to get my own copies and share them with my meeting. We used them for a year's study. All of us found them mind-blowing. In the very first lecture he reminds us that the universe has a story. It emerged from the primeval fireball, it has gone through great events. And everything that has gone before us, thirteen billion years or more of creativity on the part of the universe, was needed to bring us to this moment. The story of the universe is our story. Every child should be told:

> You come out of the energy
> that gave birth to the universe,
> it is your beginning.
> You come out of the fire
> that fashioned the galaxies
> It is alive in you.[17]

At the end of the lecture, after he had made us aware that this vast, incredible universe with its trillion galaxies, each having in the order of a hundred billion stars which are a million times larger than the earth, all came from that flaring forth of energy which began as something no bigger than a pinprick... we sat back and gasped. One of our younger Friends said 'Well, I don't understand all of it. But something deep within me says "Yes".' And I think that's what I said when I first encountered Matthew Fox and his reclamation of creation spirituality. It's what I said when I first read Thomas Berry's *Dream of the Earth* and his later book *The Great Work*. It is what I said within myself when I first saw Brian Swimme's *Canticle to the Cosmos*.

[17] Study Guide to *Canticle to the Cosmos*.

And I said, 'YES, YES, YES.' when I opened Matthew Fox's contribution to the exploration of creation spirituality and the new creation story *Sins of the Spirit, Blessings of the Flesh*. I think it is his most impressive book. In it he explores what it means to understand that we are all part of the ongoing drama of the universe, which is about 'embodiment' or 'flesh'; that we all participate in the same flesh, all derive from the same origin, and that all flesh is connected. He suggests that in our struggle to understand what this means we are being stretched and that above all, this moment of time in which we are living '... is time for soul enlargement'.[18]

---

[18] *Sins of the Spirit, Blessings of the Flesh*, p. 42.

Chapter 5
Living Earth Spirit

Alex Wildwood

Ask the animals, and they shall teach you; the birds of the air, and they shall instruct you. Speak to earth and it shall teach you.

Job 12: 7–8

Silence is indeed the Quaker way, and yet we know how very safe silence can be. Meanwhile, the great song of the Earth, once sung so eloquently by Aboriginal peoples, remains not only unsung by us because of our cultural entrapment, but also perhaps even largely unheard.

Susannah Brindle[1]

The desperate plight of our planet is bringing in its wake a revelation that is both challengingly original and yet deeply part of our ancestral wisdom. Susannah Brindle, an Australian Friend of European ancestry, has been profoundly influenced by her contact with the aboriginal peoples of the land of her birth. She is acutely aware of how as 'whitefellas' we can be trapped in 'residual fear of being branded pagan – or crazy'[2] if we feel or explore our connectedness with the Earth. She invites us to 'learn a new song' (the title of her Backhouse lecture of 2000) and so be reconciled with the Earth and its primal peoples. We are a long way from relating 'consciously and respectfully with the intelligences of the Earth, for at present we do not even acknowledge their existence':

[1] 'Quakers and the Australian Community of Nature' in *As the Seed Grows: Essays in Quaker thought* pp. 27–28. [2] *Ibid.*, p. 27.

We cannot see that at every moment we are being called to loving community with the Earth and her beings or that such engagement may be the only way forward for us all.[3]

The Dominican Sister Miriam MacGillis is one of the co-founders of Genesis Farm in New Jersey. Part of their mission statement reads: 'Genesis Farm is rooted in a belief that the Universe, Earth, and all reality are permeated by the presence and power of that ultimate Holy Mystery that has been so deeply and richly expressed in the world's spiritual traditions. We try to ground our ecological and agricultural work in this deep belief. This Sacred Mystery, known by so many religious names, is the common thread in our efforts'.[4] At a talk in London in 1998, Miriam MacGillis held aloft an image of our planet:

> You are the same as this ... You are Earth being you, just as it is being clouds, waters, wind and sycamore tree ... There is no separation, no radical discontinuity between the human and the non-human; this is our body and our blood. This is our larger self. We need to grapple with this as a grace, as a moment of revelation.[5]

Yet in the last few centuries, the dominant human cultures of the world have defined the human precisely in terms of this perceived discontinuity. We have measured cultural achievements, set our economic goals and defined religious life as if all these things were fundamentally divorced from what the poet and farmer Wendell Berry calls 'the greater economy' of the planet. We have measured human success in terms of gross national product, created nation states that have kept whole populations in poverty, and squandered vast resources in warfare and 'defence' – while creating a dangerously devitalised world.

For centuries now our culture has been engaged in creating an arrogant illusion, a fantasy world separate from the rest of nature. Conceptually and pragmatically we have rejected the biosphere (within which we are born and of which we are created) in favour of what Cormac Cullinan has named the 'homosphere' – a 'vast hermetically sealed "humans only" world' which

3 'Earth and Quakers' (Part 2), *The Australian Friend*, September 2005, p. 9. 4 www.genesisfarm.org 5 Talk given at St James's Church, Piccadilly, London, March 17th 1998: 'The New Cosmology – its implications for our lives'

fascinates us, and which with its myths of human supremacy has become more real to us than Earth itself.[6] Now, increasingly, we are forced to realise that we cannot continue to separate ourselves in this way, that this habit of isolating ourselves violates our nature and the truth of the reality we inhabit. Humanity is awakening, on an unprecedented scale, to the reality of our interdependence. And none too soon: in the words of Michael Dowd[7] in his book *EarthSpirit*, 'To think of ourselves as separate from the rest of nature, as we have, may have been important for our evolutionary development. To continue seeing ourselves this way any longer, however, is suicidal'.[8]

The cultural assumption of separation – of being apart from rather than a part of the more-than-human world – is being called into question today because of the growing evidence of the irreparable harm this thinking poses not only to our own survival but to the flourishing of life on Earth. But this shift in awareness is also being brought about because scientific enquiry has changed the way we understand physical reality, and because we are starting to see our human journey from the perspective of deep time.

Sensing what Zen poet and teacher Thich Nhat Hanh calls our 'interbeing', glimpsing how we are part of something so much vaster than our everyday sense of self, lays the foundation for a new sense of spirituality, one that resonates with the evolutionary dynamics of the Earth process itself. This emerging story of who we really are can help us lay to rest the old antagonism between religious awareness and scientific knowledge, while expanding hugely our sense of human identity – as nothing less than an aspect of the awesome evolutionary dynamic of the cosmos.[9]

The word 'shamanic' has been gaining currency among sincere spiritual seekers. Although the word has a specific anthropological meaning, it now commonly refers to an embodied awareness of the Earth as a sacred presence, to a human need to witness the passage of the seasons, to experience the elements of existence and to live in deeper connections with the rhythms of the Earth. People in industrialised nations

[6] *Wild Law* pp. 35–36. [7] www.thankgodforevolution.com/category/blog [8] *EarthSpirit: a handbook for nurturing an ecological Christianity* p. 92. [9] See www.thegreatstory.com

looking for an experiential expression of their belonging to the 'kindom' of life (a phrase coined by feminist theologian Rosemary Radford Ruether, author of the classic *Sexism and God-Talk*). They are seeking in nature a healing wisdom they can no longer find in the religion of their upbringing. Growing numbers of books, articles and experiential workshops now on offer testify to people's desire to learn from the remaining Earth-based spiritual traditions, and to seek the wisdom of the more-than-human world.[10]

I believe this poses a specific challenge to Friends – open as we say we are to 'new light from whatever source it may come'.[11] I'm aware that there is currently a great deal of soul-searching and quite some anxiety about our spiritual identity as British Quakers – particularly about whether we are moving too far from our Christian origins. While I believe it is important to be clear about who we are and what is distinctive about our Quaker Christian heritage, one of the lessons of deep time is to sit lightly with all our human labels and self-definitions. The universe story invites us to keep things in perspective!

The 'spirituality revolution' that is occurring today offers us both a tremendous challenge and a precious opportunity. How might our Quaker practices assist this shift in consciousness, how might they contribute to this emerging spirituality that so many people hunger for? But also, how might this contemporary shift in religious awareness be calling us to be more experimental, less attached to our traditional Quaker ways of doing things?

I remember as a student in the nineteen-sixties, first reading about widespread chemical pollution and being shocked to learn that detectable levels of DDT were then being found both in human breast milk and in the tissue of penguins in the Antarctic. The awareness was dawning that neither the innocence of the newborn nor the remotest reaches of our planet were immune to the ravages of industrialised humanity.

Of course, since then the understanding of our planetary ecology has developed enormously. Reflecting now on the critical scientific revolutions of the past three hundred years, I would add (after the revolutions in physics and psychology in the

10 See the magazines *Sacred Hoop, Kindred Spirit* and *Resurgence*, David Abram explores our intuitive, kinesthetic sense of being embodied in nature in *Becoming Animal: an Earthly Cosmology*. 11 *Advices & Queries* 7.

early twentieth century) the ecological revolution of the last fifty years.[12] The shift we are currently part of is every bit as radical as the shift from believing the Earth was the centre of the universe.

This ecological revolution is part of a wider shift in understanding, a move away from a preoccupation with studying isolated parts – concentrating on the separate elements of what is being studied, getting to know more and more about less and less – to a focus on the overall pattern, a consideration of *the system as a whole* and an examination of the *relationships* between the parts. This is characterised as a move from a reductionist view to one described as holistic, or systems-based approach. (Systems theory, an interdisciplinary field founded by Ludwig von Bertalanffy, William Ross Ashby and others in the 1950s, focuses on relationships of systems as a whole, and on the organisation and interdependence of relationships. Cybernetics is a closely related field of study.) Neither view is more complete or 'right' than the other; we need both for an accurate perception of reality. It is a matter of where we focus our attention – but it is also a matter of redressing the historic imbalance of concentrating on fragments in isolation: see Stephan Harding's *Animate Earth: Science, Intuition and Gaia*, which looks at how scientific rigour and subjective, intuitive responses can together give us a more accurate perception of reality.

Learning to think in terms of whole systems teaches us to look at how parts interact and how in this interacting something new, an *emergent property*, can arise. Such synergy is amusingly characterised by psychologist Chris Johnstone in his equation "1 + 1 = 2 and a bit", signalling how something more than the sum of the parts emerges in the creative dynamic of a relationship.[13] In dissecting the human body, for instance, we can locate and describe various organs, tissues and cells but we cannot locate personality in this way: personality is an emergent property of a complex organism – only intelligible in its social-psychological context. In a similar sense, life can best be understood as an emergent property of Earth's geophysical evolution.

Until very recently this has not been the accepted view. The study of the Earth has been split up into a number of different

12 I have summarised the scientific revolutions that have occurred during the 350 years of the Quaker movement in *Tradition & Transition*. 13 *Find Your Power*, p. 233

disciplines, each housed in separate buildings in our universities, with only the rare intrepid soul finding their way between them. This very architectural arrangement of higher education has long reinforced an assumed distinction between 'Earth sciences' (studying, for instance, climate and geology) and the 'Life sciences' (observing living beings that reproduce and respond to their environment). 'Psychology' (itself divided into separate compartments of clinical, development etc.) would be in another building altogether. Yet to grapple with an issue as complex as climate change and our responses to it we are going to have to break down such disciplinary boundaries.

But in the last three decades the conventional wisdom that life on Earth simply evolved in a randomly changing environment has been radically challenged by the independent scientist Professor James Lovelock. Although he has spent much of his working life based at his home in rural Devon, Lovelock developed his Gaia hypothesis while employed by NASA to develop experiments for detecting life on Mars. He saw quite early on that instead of the hugely expensive and technologically-driven way NASA was approaching things, the problem could be solved by reading the atmospheric 'signature' of Mars from here on Earth. This led him to look at what it was about the Earth's atmosphere that made life on this planet sustainable. He soon realised that if our atmosphere was made up of chemical equilibrium – as were the atmospheres of Mars and Venus – it would consist of about 98% carbon dioxide. Actually, it contains merely 0.03% carbon dioxide and 79% nitrogen – as well as 21% of the highly reactive gas oxygen.[14] This is a combination which cannot be maintained by chemical equilibrium alone.

In fact, he discovered, this very unusual combination could only have arisen and be maintained through the activities of living organisms. While his lateral thinking was initially rewarded by NASA with dismissal from the Mars project, it led to the birth of his understanding of the Earth as a living entity, where species and their environment are 'tightly coupled and evolve as a single system'.[15] He then focused on 'the evolution of the largest living organism' – for which his neighbour, the novelist William

[14] See *The Ages of Gaia*, Table 1.1, p. 9.
[15] *Ibid.*, p. xvi

Golding, suggested the mythic name Gaia, the Greek name for the Earth goddess.

About a decade before Lovelock developed his Gaia hypothesis, NASA had begun to produce the now-familiar images of the Earth from space – our small blue planet surrounded by wisps of cloud-laden atmosphere, hanging in the vast, dark immensity of space. In varied forms this image has understandably become an icon of our age, as we can now behold the wondrous integrity of our planet for the first time. Visiting Quaker meetings around the country as part of the 'Rooted in Christianity, Open to New Light' project, there was a point in my presentation on the 'new light' influencing our worldview as Friends today when I would display a large poster of this image of the Earth. There was often a gentle sigh audible in the room at that moment, a quiet recognition that in viewing this icon we may indeed experience a holy moment. Sometimes it's hard to remember that this image has only been available to us for less than fifty years.

The paradox is that this recent scientific understanding of the Earth as a living entity is by no means a new idea. In fact, it is only in the last few centuries that the educated classes of the Western world promoted the idea of our planet as essentially lifeless, an inert lump of inanimate matter orbiting around the sun, obeying purely mechanical laws. In the sixteenth and seventeenth centuries in Europe, fuelled by gold from the Americas, a merchant class emerged and with their new capitalist economy came an essentially mechanistic ideology. These new global power brokers conceived of the universe as made up of separate, lifeless parts, which could be viewed in isolation and ruthlessly exploited as resources for human use.[16]

The rise of this myth of our separation from nature seems to be strongly associated with a change at the end of the Middle Ages, in the popular image of nature. Nature was no longer seen as a nurturing mother but as a machine, or as a female body to be dominated and enslaved. This became part of the Enlightenment's view of its own tradition: Leibniz referred in 1696 to 'the art of inquiry into nature itself and of putting it on the rack – the art of experiment which Lord Bacon began

[16] For an analysis of the inter-relationship of global trade, patriarchy and attitudes to the natural world in this period, see Carolyn Merchant, *The Death of Nature: Women, ecology and the scientific revolution*, and also Brian Easlea, *Science and Sexual Oppression*.

so ably'.[17] A key figure in the new empirical exploration of the world, Bacon asserted that the purpose of science was to establish over the realm of nature 'regnum hominis', the rule or dominion of Man. (Bacon also stated that the scientist is to 'command nature ... by obeying her', but the priorities are clear for the man who is remembered for the dictum 'Knowledge is power'.[18]) Even to this day the word animistic carries pejorative connotations. Throughout the Christian era 'pagan' beliefs and practices were violently suppressed, and this demonisation was continued just as effectively by Enlightenment rationality, with continuing torture and suppression of witchcraft.

A 'paradigm shift' refers to a qualitative leap in how reality is perceived. Willis Harman, a renowned futurist, defined a paradigm in *An Incomplete Guide to the Future* as 'the basic way of perceiving, thinking, valuing and doing associated with a particular vision of reality'; Duane Elgin points out that 'A paradigm tells most people, most of the time, what's real and what's not, what's important and what's not, and how things are related to one another'.[19] So pervasive and successful was this new materialist worldview in Bacon's time that it is easy for us to forget that this ideology of nature as a 'resource' is a comparatively recent and extremely eccentric view. But given the technical prowess, imperial ambitions and enormous plundered wealth of the European nation states (and then of their descendants in North America), this paradigm of human separation has been the dominant paradigm for the last four hundred years. From the perspective of deep time, of course, this is a very new idea. The vast majority of human cultures have always experienced the Earth and all its elements and creatures as a vital, sacred presence. It can still be challenging for our post-Enlightenment minds to take on board the idea that the Earth is actually alive. Lovelock himself recognised the problem. We have been educated to think of our planetary home as simply a large ball of lifeless rock, all but the very surface of which is molten-hot and *inanimate* (literally devoid of soul), and yet 'many of the

17 Quoted by Carolyn Merchant in 'The Scientific Revolution and The Death of Nature'. 18 See Francis Bacon article at http://radicalacademy.uni.me/philfrancisbacon.htm.
19 *Promise Ahead*, p. 45.

atoms of the rocks far down into the magma were once part of the ancestral life from which we have all come'.[20]

The Gaia hypothesis challenged the deep-seated ideological assumption of separation on science's own grounds and was greeted with some derision in certain quarters as a result. Lovelock dared to step into the interdisciplinary no-man's-land where one risks getting shot at from all directions. But in a series of scientific papers, written alone and with colleagues, Lovelock turned the hypothesis into a testable theory and began to establish links between meteorology and biology. He showed how, for instance, marine algae are part of a huge system of planetary self-regulation, the global equivalent of sweating and shivering. He went on to demonstrate how in three key areas – the composition of our atmosphere, the temperature of the Earth's surface, and in the salinity of the oceans – the interaction between the physical planet Earth and the 'skin' of its life-forms and atmosphere has worked to maintain these at the exact proportions and conditions that favour life. For Lovelock, Gaia is a living organism, 'the largest of living systems' we can describe.[21]

Gaia theory has rapidly become a critical part of the ecological revolution of our time – and therefore of the larger emerging paradigm of our age – not simply because it increases our understanding of the physical world but because it feeds into a fundamental reorientation of the way we understand our relationship to the rest of life on Earth. Instead of the Biblical view of ourselves as having been given 'dominion over … every living thing that moves upon the earth'[22] we now have to consider that being 'made in the image of God' does not mean a mandate to control or dominate, but points us towards an ancient relational identity, a sense of ourselves as necessarily embedded within the greater body of Earth-life – an ecological integrity that we deny at our peril. Ecological laws, we are discovering, are quite as fundamental and binding as the laws of physics.

In his choice of the name Gaia, James Lovelock managed to combine scientific enquiry with religious instinct. He described his own rural upbringing as 'an odd mixture, composed of witches, May trees, and the views expressed by Quakers, in and

---

[20] *Ages of Gaia*, p. 27. [21] *Ibid.*, p. 215.
[22] Genesis 1:36 New Revised Standard Version.

outside the Sunday school at a Friends' meeting house'.[23] These influences combined to give him a sense that life cannot be separated into sacred and secular parts. 'Living itself is a religious experience', he affirms; insistence on credal professions of faith can 'anaesthetise the sense of wonder'.[24] Contrary to what some critics suppose, he does not see Gaia as a sentient being, a surrogate God. But he does accept that Gaia is inevitably 'a religious as well as a scientific concept', which he finds 'deeply satisfying'.[25]

While Lovelock has continued to elaborate Gaia theory solely within his own discipline of science, others have not felt so constrained. Two-thirds of the correspondence he has received since first proposing the Gaia hypothesis have been about the meaning of Gaia in the context of religious faith. For such people, the mythic name of Gaia speaks powerfully of the spirit of our times in evoking a different kind of worldview, one that embraces the long-forgotten feminine and which honours the matrix of life and its fecundity in an overtly spiritual way. In using the name of Gaia, Lovelock tapped into a potent cultural archetype, an antidote to the patriarchal sky God, at the historical moment when hundreds of thousands of women (and a minority of men) – in Europe, America, Australia and New Zealand – felt led to explore a spiritual vision that affirmed their experience and their sense of being a part of nature and its rhythms of birth, death and renewal. Gaia was one more fitting image of female power and nurturance. A book that captured this new approach was *The Spiral Dance: a rebirth of the ancient religion of the Great Goddess*, by Starhawk, a self-proclaimed modern witch.

I remember the controversy there was in the Yearly Meeting session when we considered the inclusion of the one entry in the current edition of *Quaker Faith & Practice* that makes reference to the word 'Goddess' (section 26.35 by Rose Ketterer, who writes it 'G–d/ess' – which 'attempts to convey the difficulty of naming the divine', the dash being 'an old Jewish practice meant to show the impossibility of conveying the divine in a word'). It was sobering to hear how challenging this was for some present. For others of us, it really wasn't an issue. The word itself signifies

[23] *Ages of Gaia*, p. 204.　[24] *Ibid.*, pp. 204–5.　[25] *Ibid.*, p. 206.

how many today feel called to explore a feminine sense of sacred mystery, of ultimate reality, rooted in the Earth and its cycles and seasons, explored in ways that embrace and validate both their bodily experience and more intuitive ways of knowing. One of the most articulate leaders of those exploring the religion of the Goddess, Starhawk, speaks of the Goddess as a symbol which emphasises the positive use of female power 'to create a world where the Earth and all its people live in harmony and peace'. For her it makes sense to speak of the creative power at the heart of life in this way:

> ...the Goddess is the name we put on the great processes of birth, growth, death and regeneration that underlie the living world ... the presence of consciousness in all living beings ... the great creative force that spun the universe out of coiled strings of probability and set the stars spinning and dancing in spirals that our entwining DNA echoes as it coils, uncoils, and evolves.[26]

The term "thealogy" began to appear in feminist literature of the neopagan Goddess movement during the 1980s; the original use of the word is attributed to both Isaac Bonewits and Naomi R Goldenberg – the latter using the term in her 1979 book *Changing of the Gods: feminism and the end of traditional religions*. The basis of traditional religious life has been upside down, such 'thealogians' argue. We have imagined a God made in the image of the human and have projected male (feudal and monarchical) values onto 'Him' to create a fearsome Lord, a judging Father deity. Many women speak today of a very different sense of the divine, and naturally use Goddess language to do so. (The literature on 'Goddess' in language, symbol and ritual is too extensive to summarise here: see, for instance, *Womanspirit rising: a feminist reader* and Carol Christ and Judith Plaskow's excellent *Rebirth of the Goddess: Finding meaning in feminist spirituality*.)

From the earliest of human artefacts, there is evidence of the Earth being reverenced as a goddess, and the myth of the Great Mother seems to have been part of many early religions. This mythic Mother is a compassionate, feminine figure, the font of all life and fecundity. But she is also the harsh and relentless bearer of death. Lovelock recalls the image of Kali in

[26] *The Earth Path*, p. 5.

the Hindu tradition – the infinitely kind and loving mother and terrifying Goddess of destruction: the life-bestower also requires us to embrace death, that life must end in death and is renewed through death.

Less than five thousand years ago, the concept of 'a remote, master God, an overseer of Gaia' took root in human consciousness. Charlene Spretnak in her book *The Spiritual Dimension of Green Politics*, sees this as the moment that Gaia, the prior deity, was first deposed. From the archaeological record we can imagine that decisive moment about 4,500 years BCE when horsemen from the east invaded south-eastern Europe, bringing with them 'a sky god, a warrior cult, and patriarchal social order'.[27]

Clearly, we cannot recapture or recreate a lost past, but many people today feel called to live from the same sense of reverence for the Earth as earlier human cultures seem to have done. They want to practise the same appreciation of the Earth as a sacred, living, entity – the visible manifestation of the divine mystery, worthy of our deepest respect. Starhawk and other contemporary pagans show how the primal religious impulse was our ancestors' 'actual relationship to a specific place on earth':

> And the tools of magic, that discipline of identifying and shifting consciousness, were the skills of listening to what ethnobotanist Kat Harrison calls 'the great conversation', the ongoing constant communication that surrounds us.[28]

It is from this primal relationship – and then from our human social relations that develop from this – that our conceptions of the divine grow.

Of course, most of us now live in cities, we read, write, use our cars and computers, we live our lives quite oblivious to this surrounding conversation. Starhawk certainly speaks to my condition when she writes: 'We may love nature, we may even profess to worship her, but most of us have barely a clue as to what she is murmuring in the night'.[29]

Unsurprisingly perhaps, the yearning for an expression of our sacred ecology, a spiritual expression of our interconnectedness, is arising as more and more people around the world move into

27 *The Spiritual Dimension of Green Politics*, quoted in *Ages of Gaia*, p. 209.
28 *The Earth Path* p. 7. 29 *Ibid.*

cities, losing touch – literally – with the rhythms and seasons of the natural world. Cut off from this 'great conversation' of the more-than-human world, we are spiritually in jeopardy. For while some science-fiction writers imagine the technopolis of the future, a domed 'homosphere' with controlled climate and genetically engineered populations, for the truly prophetic voices of our time this is a dangerous illusion. We are born of this Earth, cradled in its life-systems, formed by its beauty and specific wonders. The central message of Thomas Berry's ministry over the past four decades has been that our embeddedness in nature is *a spiritual truth* as well as a factual, physical reality. As in his video *The Great Story*, his religious vision is of humanity birthed out of, and totally dependent upon, this integral evolutionary matrix.

For pioneering human ecologist Paul Shepard, the self is 'ennobled and extended rather than threatened as part of the landscape and the ecosystem, because the beauty and complexity of nature are continuous with ourselves',[30] and as he has poignantly put it, 'The others have made us human'.[31] What James Lovelock and collaborators worldwide have achieved is to give a scientific rationale, a sound intellectual basis, to our intuitive sense of interconnectedness. Biology Professor Lynn Margulis is seldom credited with her role in helping Lovelock shape his original Gaia hypothesis. She remained a critical ally, seeing the Earth as an interdependent ecosystem, not a living organism.[32] Acknowledging that we derive our existence – personal, physical, and spiritual – from the integrity of the Earth as a living system is an idea whose time has come. If the potential for an Earth-centred spirituality is to take us beyond 'the heresy of humanism', then the difficulty we immediately encounter is that our dominant faith traditions have, by and large, been fashioned by doctrines of an anthropomorphic God.

According to Douglas Watt, a neuropsychologist at the Boston University School of Medicine, we are 'powerfully neurologically

[30] 'Ecology and Man', in Shepard and McKinley, eds, *The Subversive Science*. [31] *Nature and Madness;* quoted by Roger Gottlieb, 'Spiritual Deep Ecology and World Religions: a Shared Fate, a Shared Task', in *Deep Ecology and World Religions*, p. 19. [32] See her 'Gaia is tough bitch', www.edge.org/documents/ThirdCulture/n-Ch.7.html

primed to generate this anthropomorphism of God' because
of the long period of human infantile dependence, and 'the
manner in which any concept of value (let alone any concept of
ultimate value) is inherently and inextricably bound to images
of caregivers'. This notion of 'God as Person', he concludes is
'perhaps the ultimate, and most deceptive and seductive, form
of idolatry'. In this sense, the 'death of God' phenomenon in
the West during the twentieth century can be seen as part of our
spiritual coming of age, a vital part of our initiation in this time
of transition. Douglas Watt shows why this is such a challenge, for
the 'loss of the magical kingdom of infancy and early childhood
is a most difficult bit of reality to swallow'.[33] Yet any real bridging
between religious faith and what science reveals to us about the
nature of reality and the Universe requires a shift away from
this sense of God as personage – a concept deeply ingrained in
'the religions of the Book'. The paradox is that we are called
to a deeply personal relationship with Mystery, yet this intimacy
is not with a Being amongst other beings. In realising that we
are formed, literally, from stardust, that the heavier elements
(required in complex compounds necessary for life) are created
in the interior of stars that go supernova, we are put in touch
with a religious sense of awe and wonder. In the full realisation of
this, science and faith can mutually enrich each other.[34]

When Jo and I led a weekend on 'Faith in Transition' at
Charney Manor in 2006 – on the implications of the new universe
story for religious faith – one participant wrote a moving poem
that ended with the lines:

Is the darkness full or empty
Is there anybody there?
Or is it the echo
of my own voice
crying
that I hear?[35]

She had earlier, in great honesty, shared that for her the new
story of our origins brought up not intellectual denial – hard as

33 'Attachment Mechanisms and the Bridging of Science and Religion' in *Ways of Knowing* (ed. Chris Clarke) p. 77. 34 *Ibid.*, p. 80.
35 Lynn Jennings, 'Creation spirituality – a response' [unpublished]

the real comprehension of light years and galaxies is to grasp – but 'a raw pulsating fear' that made her want to run and hide. Coming of age theologically, though essential, is not necessarily going to be easy.

To get beyond the anthropomorphic and androcentric notions of God of our tradition and return to a more Earth-centred religious awareness, is also, in important ways to return to our roots.

Back in the 1960s, Lynn White Jnr. sparked a fierce debate with his controversial article, 'The Historical Roots of Our Ecological Crisis',[36] in which he argued that Jewish and Christian 'desacralization' of the Earth and nature paved the way for our modern attitudes of domination and 'radical separation' from the rest of Earth-life. White claimed that, 'especially in its Western form, Christianity is the most anthropocentric religion the world has seen'. He proposed the radical St Francis as a patron saint for ecologists, because he advocated the virtue of humility, not merely for individuals but for mankind as a species. But White was only too aware that Francis failed in his attempt to redirect the Christian tradition in this way.

The very idea of 'sacred nature' has been anathema to most forms of Christianity (the exception being the panentheism of Celtic Christianity) – and therefore to the worldview of the West. This wariness of anything 'pagan' is also found among Friends, of course. See, for instance, 'Christian Earth Stewardship' by Steven Davison in the most comprehensive Quaker document on concern for the Earth, the 1994 anthology Becoming a Friend to the Creation: Earthcare Leaven for Friends and Friends' Meetings, published by Friends Committee on Unity with Nature. In his '9½ Principles of Christian Earth Stewardship', the very first is 'Creation is good but not holy'.[37] A more nuanced approach is given by Keith Helmuth who, in examining 'The Market Economy as a Spiritual Concern', writes 'Creation is unique among our concepts; it has no opposite ... Creation teaches us ultimacy; it is the source of our sense of the sacred'.[38]

[36] First published in *Science*, Vol 155, #3767, 10 March 1967, pp. 1203–1207, reprinted in *This Sacred Earth*, ed. Roger S. Gottlieb.
[37] *Becoming a Friend to the Creation* p. 58. [38] *Ibid.*, p. 80.

As we humble ourselves in the face of the ineffable mystery of divine presence encountered in the more-than-human world, Susannah Brindle suggests that it is precisely 'our faith in scientific rationalism' and our 'quaint notion that humanity shares Spirit with the Divine, exclusively', that may have to go.[39] Yet this could actually be part of a reanimation of the Religious Society of Friends, at a time when as a faith community we have been deeply influenced by the post-Enlightenment, secular world around us; as Friends and attenders we seem increasingly uncomfortable to speak of 'Spirit' (a term more widely used by British Friends than the word 'God' today). What do we actually mean by the term, Brindle asks:

> Is our Spirit more of a culturally crafted concept, an unembodied sanction for what we have come to think is the kindest, most just, most loving, most practical way to be or think to do? Or is our Spirit a Force of incomprehensible, unfathomable, unimaginable Love, Creation and Destruction – moulding our unwilling lives all too uncomfortably at times and having us occasionally glimpse an understanding that we … may not constitute the spiritual pinnacle and centre of Creation after all?[40]

She sees the great potential of what Patricia Loring calls a Quaker 'listening spirituality' today, as a dialogue, to 'listen to and converse with earth'.Although as a culture we have lost the capacity of 'speaking to the Earth and the animals who will teach us',[41] Brindle sees meeting for worship having the potential to lead us from our cultural 'comfort blanket' of scientific rationality to where we will be 'given a wiser and more inclusive view of Life's Drama' and be reminded that 'rather than occupying centre-stage … we are required to play supporting roles'.[42]

Lyn White saw the paradox of our situation. Our present science and technologies, he argued, are 'so tinctured with orthodox Christian arrogance toward nature' that they cannot supply the answers we need. Yet:

> Since the roots of our trouble are so largely religious, the remedy must be essentially religious, whether we call it that

39 'Earth and Quakers, part 1', *The Australian Friend*, March 2005, p. 15. 40 *Ibid.*, p. 8. 41 Job 12:1–8. 42 'Earth and Quakers, part 2', *The Australian Friend*, September 2005, p. 8.

or not. We must rethink and refeel our nature and destiny.[43]

The challenge we face is to break out of that limited sense of self promoted by both secular psychologies and traditional Christian doctrines. We need to experience in this time a larger identity – a process Joanna Macy calls 'the Greening of the Self'. Contemporary revelations of science – together with certain kinds of religious awareness (especially from Buddhism) are combining to challenge our Western philosophical assumption of a distinct, separate, continuous self. What a true appreciation of our interdependence teaches us is that 'there is no logical or scientific basis for construing one part of the experienced world as "me" and the rest as "other"'. In an interconnected, evolving universe, Macy points out, 'integration and differentiation go hand in hand'. She acknowledges that what she calls the 'ecological self' is itself only another metaphorical construct, but it is a dynamic one. We have the choice

> To identify at different moments, with different dimensions or aspects of our systemically interrelated existence – be they hunted whales or homeless humans or the planet itself. In doing this the extended self brings into play wider resources – courage, endurance, ingenuity – like a nerve cell in a neural net opening to the charge of the other neurons.[44]

Informed by such a perspective, Starhawk offers a suggestion for the kind of religious practices urgently needed today, a plea for an engaged spirituality that may resonate with many Friends:

> Instead of closing our eyes to meditate, we need to open our eyes and observe. Unless our spiritual practice is grounded in a real connection to the natural world, we run the risk of simply manipulating our own internal imagery and missing the real communication taking place all around us.[45]

Our 'coming back to life' – as Joanna Macy names the challenge of our age[46] will mean a fundamental change in our ideas

[43] 'The Historical Roots of our Ecological Crisis', in *Science*, vol. 155 no. 3767 (March 10, 1967). [44] 'The Greening of the Self', in *World as Lover, World as Self*, pp. 183–192. [45] *The Earth Path*, p. 11. [46] Joanna Macy & Molly Young Brown, *Coming Back to Life: Practices to reconnect our lives, our world*.

of the relationship between ourselves and nature, and this will depend, as Lynn White foresaw back in the 1960s, on whether we can 'find a new religion or rethink our old one'.[47]

For many of us today, rethinking and refeeling that relationship needs to include practices that honour our connectedness with the Earth as a sacred reality. The religious life, as the Quaker movement has consistently asserted, is defined not by doctrines or creeds but by embodied experience and practical expressions of service and witness. Our future celebrations and ceremonies may remain as simple as a meeting for worship, but they may well need to take us out of the meeting house:

> When we feel confused or become lost in complex abstractions, it is important not to forget to go back to the beginning and connect once more with our common ground. To walk wet-footed in the cold grass of dawn, to breathe clean air, and turn the rough surfaces of a stone in our hands, until we remember who we are and why this is important.[48]

[47] Lynn White, 'The Historical Roots of our Ecological Crisis'.
[48] Cormac Cullinan, *Wild Law*, p. 233.

Chapter 6
That's the Spirit!

Jo Farrow

> I know that my hunger to return, again and again, to the mountains, to the rivers and streams, to the trees and meadows, is a hunger for the Spirit. The forests are temples for me.
>
> Bruce Birchard[1]

> The task of the spirit was always to give life. In this ancient understanding, the spiritual person was not the pious person or the religious person, but the vital, alive, whole and real person.
>
> John Shelby Spong[2]

Some years ago I facilitated a Conference in the Lake District, for Yorkshire Friends, on the theme of 'The Holy Spirit'. At the beginning of the weekend, as a warm-up exercise and a mini-introduction to the theme I suggested that we all design a T-shirt to tell one another some of the important things about ourselves. We had lot of brightly coloured crayons and felt pens, and large sheets of paper, which we later pinned on our chests. I suggested that we draw pictograms or visual symbols of things that gave us pleasure and enjoyment, things that made us feel most awake and passionately alive, those things that had the 'tingle-factor' for us.

It was a revealing exercise in many ways. Very few Friends drew anything to symbolise 'worship' as giving them frissons of delight! Restrained Anglo-Saxons that we were, no one drew any

[1] *The Burning One-ness Binding Everything*, p. 7
[2] *Why Christianity Must Change or Die*, p. 105

symbols about making love. Sadly, nobody put symbols for the work they did for a living. But most Friends did, in fact, put things they really enjoyed – walking in the country, sailing, swimming, travel, gardening, making music, a glass of wine, reading a good book, being with friends – a host of things like that. Towards the end of the session a man got up and protested, 'You can't seriously be equating the Holy Spirit with the "tingle-factor" can you?' Remembering that in the section on 'The Holy Spirit' in the *Methodist Hymn Book*, there is a favourite hymn of mine by George Macdonald, with the line – 'whatever wakes my heart and mind, Thy presence is, my Lord' – I took a deep breath and said 'Yes'.

In his book *The Household of God*, Lesslie Newbigin suggests that there are three distinct forms of Christianity. There may well be more, but he lists 1) The Congregation of the Faithful, which he identifies as the Protestant option, 2) The Body of Christ, which he sees as the Catholic option, and 3) The Community of the Spirit, which he understands as the Pentecostal version. Perhaps he saw Quakers as simply the extreme end of the Protestant Reformation, but there are significant ways in which we do not fit easily into the Protestant model. The Bible and 'the Preaching of the Word' are not central to our form of worship. We have refused the option of a separated ministry, though this is not true of all Quaker communities in other parts of the world. Our worship, at least in Britain Yearly Meeting, is without the distinctive features of most forms of Protestant worship, whether liturgical or of the 'hymn-prayer-reading-sandwich' variety. Douglas Steere described Quaker Meetings as 'laboratories of the Holy Spirit'.[3] I want to identify Friends as belonging to the 'Community of the Spirit' version of the Church.

In the Quaker understanding of Church order and government it is the Spirit who is seen as the leader of the faithful community. It is clear that George Fox and the first generation of Friends believed that, in the promise and intention of Jesus, a new community of faith was inaugurated, a new age begun, in which the Spirit would be their inward tutor and guide. In their understanding of continuous revelation it was the Spirit who would always be their contemporary, continually leading them into new truth.

[3] *Quaker Spirituality*, p. 15

In one sense George Fox got it right, but in another he got it terribly wrong. *But it wasn't his fault:* he was following the long tradition of the Western churches in the way they identified the work of the Spirit. For him, and for them, the Spirit was the 'Spirit of Jesus'. Fox used a variety of terms to describe the inward work of the Spirit. Sometimes he spoke of the Christ in the heart. Sometimes he talked about the Seed of God or the Inward Light, but these were all ways of speaking about the Christ within, because for him that was who the Spirit was. He saw people being convinced, and allowing the Light to show up the dark places in their lives, and he said, in effect, 'That's the Spirit'. He saw Friends growing in holiness and said, 'That's the Spirit', because that was how the Western church had generally identified the Holy Spirit, as doing the work of salvation and sanctification among those who were believers, or bringing sinners to repentance.

We need to do some Church history at this point to understand how the shift occurred from an inclusive understanding of the life-giving Spirit of God to an exclusive view of the Spirit as only at work in the Church, or in bringing people into the community of faith. We have to flashback to the year 1054, because that's the year of the Great Schism between the Eastern Orthodox Church and Western Catholicism. In many ways it was a much more devastating splitting off than the Protestant Reformation. One reason for the split had to do with power struggles between the Patriarch of Constantinople and the Pope, but much of it hinged on what it actually meant when you said 'That's the Spirit'.

The Western churches saw the Spirit at work in the Church, in narrow religious terms, convincing would-be believers of their sin, bringing them to a reliance on the saving work of Jesus and leading them on in the way of holiness. His role in all of this was subordinate. The Spirit was the Spirit brokered for the faithful by Jesus himself. That's how George Fox, whose knowledge of Church history was slight, and decidedly biased, saw it.

But the Churches of the East had quite a different view. They saw the Spirit in universal terms, as the Spirit of Life, the Spirit of God, flowing through the whole of Creation, giving life to everything in the universe. It was not primarily 'the Spirit of Jesus' and it was not subordinate in any way, and they were on much firmer ground. The words translated as 'Spirit' in our Bibles, *ruach* in the Hebrew Old Testament, *pneuma* in the Greek New Testament, literally means 'breath'. And 'breath' means life. If you stop breathing you die. So the Spirit was the life-giver. Even in English we have a number of words that carry that particular meaning. We talk about a lively performance as a 'spirited' one. We speak of something that makes us feel invigorated and uplifted as something that is 'inspiring'. If the same thing is flat and not at all lively, we say it was 'uninspiring'. If someone is sad and depressed we may say that they are 'dispirited'. It all comes from the same root and means the same thing – the difference between what is lively and what is lifeless.

Today we know much more about the miracle of 'breath'. John Gribbin, author of the book to accompany the 2001 BBC series 'Space', writes: 'If you take a deep breath you will have more molecules of air in your lungs than there are stars in all the galaxies in the visible universe put together'.[4] David Suzuki, the acclaimed geneticist and environmentalist, in his book *The Sacred Balance* observes that in our everyday life we breathe in atoms from the air that were once part of birds, trees, snakes and worms, and the longer we live the more likely it is that we will absorb atoms that were once part of the first human beings, from woolly mammoths, from Jesus, from our forebears: 'Air is the matrix that joins all life together ... We are bound inseparably with the past and the future by the spirit we share ... Every breath is a sacrament, an affirmation of our connection with all other living things, a renewal of our link with our ancestors and a contribution to generations yet to come. Our breath is part of life's breath.'[5] The traditional Benediction that closes with the phrase 'the fellowship of the Holy Spirit' is actually alluding to a reality so vast that no human being could begin to imagine it.

Ruach could also mean 'wind' in the sense that the wind blowing is invigorating and refreshing. Anyone who has taught small children will know what happens to them on a windy day. On a really windy day even our two cats race round the house as if super-charged with energy. As we say of someone who comes

4 *Space*, p. 21. 5 *The Sacred Balance*, p. 49

into a situation and somehow livens it up, that he or she is 'like a breath of fresh air'. So the Spirit, as 'breath' or 'wind', is the invigorator, the one who brings new life into a situation, as well as the breath or spirit that connects us with everything in the universe, everything and everyone that has ever been and everything that is to come.

Jurgen Moltmann is a leading theologian who has made a special study of the Holy Spirit in the life of the Church, in the life of the world, in our ordinary human experiences and in the fabric of the Universe itself. I have returned to his work again and again because he is one of the few theologians who has explored this area with any thoroughness. He laments the fact that in the Western churches the Spirit came to be seen as some kind of supernatural agent operating chiefly in ecclesiastic circles, bound to the institutions of the church, to the conventional stages in the development of faith in the believer, and mediated through the offices and rituals of the church and the instruction of its properly accredited spiritual pastors and teachers. The early Quakers rebelled against this, of course, and put a premium on the inward teacher and the experience of the individual. But it was still in the strictly religious experiences of convincement, repentance, turning to the Light and being made holy or perfect, that they saw the Spirit at work.

No wonder, then, that in his major theological study of the 'spirit' Jürgen Moltmann emphasises the fact that God's Spirit is not the special possession of the religious. It is the creative, energising, revitalising Spirit of Life itself. He argues that since God's spirit fills the world, 'It is therefore possible to experience God in, with and beneath each everyday experience of the world'.[6] He points out that a mutation took place when theologians made the move from the Hebrew *ruach* – the life-giving spirit of God, which was feminine, and was applied inclusively to the energy flowing through the universe giving life to everything – to *pneuma tou theou* which was neuter, and becoming much more narrowly religious, and finally to *Spiritus Sanctus*, which was masculine and very definitely describing something exclusively religious, fenced off and apart from ordinary human life, which was the way in which George Fox and seventeenth-century Friends

[6] *Spirit of Life*, p. 34

understood it when they saw themselves living in a new age of the Spirit. They were not into the 'otherworldly' versions of life in the Spirit, but they certainly accepted in the main, the version that emerged after the split away from the Orthodox Church in 1054 when the church in the West insisted on a subordinate status for the Holy Spirit.

If we want to understand what *ruach* means, Moltmann urges us to forget the word 'spirit' as it has been written about in Western culture.[7] The Greek word *pneuma*, the Latin *spiritus* and the German *geist* (and, of course, the English 'Holy Ghost') were all conceived as the opposite of matter and body, the opposite of earth and earthy. They meant something disembodied and supernatural. They were, in part, responsible for the Western church elevating spirit and putting down the body, and dividing spirituality and sensuousness. We have to wrestle with what this means for us as Quakers, since this was how George Fox and early Friends understood the indwelling Christ, the Seed and the Inward Light and this has deeply influenced our understanding of worship and Church Order.

In the Preface to 'Spirit of Life', Jürgen Moltmann acknowledged his debt to feminist and ecology students. He was aware that the quiet revolution in women's understanding of spirituality was beginning to reverse the movement away from *ruach* and reclaiming spirituality as creative vitality and connectedness to the whole of life. Nelle Morton, in her research into the history of the word 'spirit' points out that it is even older than *ruach*. She traces it back to Goddess history, to the great Earth Mother, the source of all living creatures, who breathes the creative energy of life into everything, the One in whom we all 'live and move and have our being'.

The real meaning of *ruach* as 'breath of life' came home to me when I was leaving New Zealand after the month of running workshops on Spirituality, in which it became clear to me that men as well as women were in search of a new, or re-discovering an old, earth-centred vision. As I left, at the close of the Friends Easter Gathering at Wanganui, which is Maori country, some of the participants in the weekend came to me, put their arms round me and 'hongied' me. If you were to see two Maori people doing it in greeting or farewell you might think they were

7 *Spirit of Life*, p. 40

just rubbing noses. But in fact pressing your nose against that of another human being and holding it there is a symbol of the fact that you are exchanging the breath of life with one another. You are breathing life into the one you are meeting or leaving. And it is a symbolic reminder of the Great Earth Mother or the Great Spirit who breathes life into the whole creation.

Perhaps that should be the question we set over against all our spiritual practices and communities, 'Do they give us the breath of life, do they breathe life into us, enliven us – or are they dispiriting, depressing or deadening?' And, equally important, do we see ourselves as a distinctive community of the Spirit in its narrow religious sense, 'a special people' over against other less enlightened communities, or do we understand that, as Moltmann insists, 'the cosmic breadth of God's Spirit' leads us in the opposite direction – 'to respect for the dignity of all created things, in which God is present through his Spirit'.[8]

When Christopher Holdsworth gave the 1985 Swarthmore Lecture, he gave it the title *Steps in A Large Room*, adapted from a verse in Psalm 31. He used the Coverdale translation that was familiar to him from the Book of Common Prayer. The New English Bible translates it as 'but thou hast set me free to range at will'. The New Revised Standard Version also has 'You have set my feet in a broad place'. The Authorised Version, close to the Prayer Book Version, has 'Thou hast set my feet in a large room'. The Good News Bible translates it 'you have given me freedom to go where I wish'. All of these translations are based on the conviction that the life-giving Spirit of God gives people space.

Jürgen Moltmann echoes this when he suggests that the Hebrew word for Spirit (*ruach*) was probably related to the word *rewah* meaning 'breadth'. So the Spirit creates space. It leads us out of narrow spaces. He says that to experience the sacred or the divine is not only an encounter with something personal, or with a force. It is also an experience of being given space. 'According to Kabbalistic Jewish tradition, one of God's secret names is *Makom*, the wide space'.[9]

Many people today have voted with their feet and walked away from the Church or any kind of formal religion because they believe that there is something narrow and constraining about religious institutions. Some have walked away from Quaker

[8] *Spirit of Life*, p. 10. [9] *Ibid.*, p. 43.

Meetings for the same reason. But Moltmann is suggesting that in the Hebrew understanding of *ruach* the opposite is true. God's Spirit is a 'broad open space' that allows us as human beings to find the freedom to be ourselves.

So we need to ask 'what does it really mean to be a "Community of the Spirit"? It must at the very least mean that the meeting is a lively one. When I spent a great deal of time travelling among Friends and visiting many different meetings I was often struck by the fact that some meetings had an atmosphere of depression about them. Others impressed me, almost as soon as I crossed the threshold of the meeting house, as lively and vigorous. I seem to recollect that the American psychiatrist, Alice Miller, has observed that the opposite of depression is not gaiety, but vitality.

It also suggests that our Meetings should be the kind of gatherings that encourage us to be as fully and truthfully ourselves as possible, that we give one another the space to be who we are without the pressure to conform to some idealised notion of what Quakers should be like. This is particularly important in a faith community like the Society of Friends where the pressures to conform can sometimes seem enormous. Since we have no credal basis we have no official orthodoxy of belief, but we do have what Pink Dandelion calls our 'orthopraxis'.[10] That constitutes a huge pressure to measure up to whatever is judged to be proper Quaker practice. There have been, as I have suggested, a number of surveys of the Society of Friends in recent years, and even one or two Swarthmore Lectures, which seem to be saying to us 'You are not good enough'. They seemed to be suggesting that we are not sufficiently like our seventeenth century ancestors, or that somehow we ought to be John Woolman look-alikes or clones of Elizabeth Fry.

There are many things about George Fox that I find difficult but I warm to the side of him that emerges in his pastoral letters to Friends. In spite of his passionate concern for 'perfection', he was wise about human beings and their limitations. His letters are often very down to earth in advising Friends not to go beyond their measure, by which he meant 'live out the bit of truth and insight that is yours and don't try to go beyond it. Don't try to run in the Light before you can walk in it'. In other words, when

10 A *Sociological Analysis of the Theology of Quakers*, p. 299

Friends began to indulge in a bit of spiritual one-upmanship he urged them to desist. If they felt the urge to some grand and heroic gesture he pleaded with them to 'stand still' and wait until they were clear that this was really a genuine prompting of the Spirit rather than a bit of spiritual showing off. And above all he advises Friends not to attempt to imitate one another.[11]

Jean Vanier, the founder of the L'Arche communities has a lot to say about real community as the place where we are liberated to be ourselves. He discovered that the biggest obstacles to growth were that those involved in the L'Arche communities had great difficulty in trusting themselves. He writes: "We can so quickly feel that we are not lovable, that if others saw us as we really are they would reject us. We are afraid of all that is darkness in ourselves".[12] He goes on to say that genuine community enables people to discover and love their uniqueness. They find the courage to be themselves, not having to live according to the desires or pressures of others, or even their own image of how they should be. He confesses that he has always wanted to write a book called 'The Right to be a Rotter' or perhaps more accurately, 'The Right to be Oneself". He observes that one of the real difficulties about community life is the pressure we put on others to be what they are not, to present them with an ideal to which they feel they ought to conform. 'So they feel obliged to hide behind a mask ... community is not about perfect people. It is about people bonded to each other, each of whom is a mixture of good and bad, darkness and light, love and hate. And community is the only earth in which each can grow without fear towards the liberation of the forces of love which are hidden in them'.[13]

Having the courage to be yourself is also dependent on another kind of necessary but unspectacular kind of courage – that of learning to love the whole of yourself, the weakness as well as the strength, the darkness as well as the light, the awkwardness as well as the grace. For, of course, those parts of ourselves that we may see as ugly or negative or shameful are precisely those that need the most love. If we cannot love the poor and afflicted parts of ourselves with a real and generous sympathy and respect

---

[11] Epistles 4, 16, 35, 41, 47, 51, 63, 79, 83, 118; in *No More but My Love*, pp. 2, 8, 17, 18, 21, 23, 29, 36, 38, 50.
[12] *Community and Growth*, p. 41. [13] *Ibid.*, pp. 42–43

we are not likely to be able to love others at all well. We may be able to feel pity or concern, but love and respect, which are the only things that don't diminish another person; we shall not be able to manage.

To be a community of the Spirit, then, is to be a vital and invigorating one and one that allows each member the space to be who they are. So the questions we might ask about our meetings could be: 'Are they full of life and really inspiring? Do the things that happen in them help us to celebrate life and live it to the full? Do we experience the Spirit as a compelling and powerful incentive to change, to go beyond the conventional? Do they also give us space and the freedom to be ourselves, not hemmed in or cramped by pressures to be a certain kind of person, rather than encouraging us to become more and more truly ourselves?'

I don't mean that Quaker Meetings should become 'clap-happy' gatherings, with everyone smiling inanely like presenters of 'Songs of Praise', or that they should be full of Spiritual Hippies dancing round the Meeting room with a flower behind each ear. I do mean that there should be something about them that helps us to say a full-blooded 'Yes' to life, rather than occasions when we sink into a serene oblivion in order to escape from its pressures and challenges. The Celtic symbol of the Spirit is not the Dove, but the Wild Goose, and I believe a community of the Spirit is one in which we should expect sometimes to be in touch with that part of ourselves that was once nomadic and undomesticated, the part of us that is willing to be pushed out into the unknown or compelled to take some new and risky venture of faith. In her James Backhouse Lecture, Susannah Brindle observes, 'Knowing this Spirit experimentally is to live perpetually on the edge, where one is constantly challenged and facing change'.[14]

One of the people who have written and spoken most insistently about the Spirit as the giver of life, calling us to a passionate and juicy enjoyment of life at that, is Matthew Fox. He has been concerned to recover the Hebrew and Eastern Churches' understanding of the Spirit as the creative and renewing energy of God flowing through the whole universe, enlivening all things, bringing new life out of death and destruction, giving the space for human beings to breathe freely and become fully themselves.

14 *To Learn a New Song*, p. 38.

He has battled energetically against the obsession of the Western church with the doctrines of Fall and Atonement and written instead of the lost and forgotten aspects of the Christian tradition that have to do with life as blessing. To combat the Western churches' preoccupation with the doctrine of 'Original Sin', he wrote his best-known book, *Original Blessing*.

In the second chapter of that book he writes about 'Creation as Blessing and the Recovery of the Art of Savouring Pleasure'. He suggests that the Doctrine of Original Sin came about from a foolishly literal interpretation of the Genesis creation story, and from St. Augustine's personal hang-ups about the sins of sexuality, his hatred of the body and of women as temptresses. He writes about the harm this has done to human beings through this quite unbiblical notion that we come into the world as further blotches on an already corrupt creation.

This was, of course, the prevailing religious idea when our Quaker story began. It may have been partly to counteract the idea that human beings would always be tainted and flawed in this life that George Fox went overboard in the opposite direction and claimed that it was possible to be perfect and without sin if only human beings allowed themselves to be fully open to the Spirit. It was also the result of his overwhelming experience of seeing the world with new eyes and believing that he had been transported back to Eden to walk and talk with God as Adam had done before the Fall. It was an over-reaction (and one that eventually had to be modified), and a misapprehension of the Genesis myth, but it was understandable. George Fox had been to hell and back in struggling to throw off the oppressive, sin-sodden weight of his Calvinistic upbringing.

Also in *Original Blessing*, Matthew Fox says:

> If creation is a blessing and a constantly original one, then our proper response would be to enjoy it. Pleasure is one of the deepest experiences of our lives. Ecstasy is the experience of God ... The true contemplative will teach us the art of savouring.[15]

As Quakers, whose form of silent worship gives us a marvellous opportunity to learn the habit of reflection and the art of contemplation, it may be that being 'Communities of the Spirit' in

[15] *Original Blessing*, pp. 45–52.

the twenty-first century requires us to learn and teach the 'art of savouring'. Certainly we need to look at how far the ethos of our meetings encourages us to see pleasure and a rich enjoyment of life as necessary nourishment for our spiritual life; and also how far it allows us enough time to recover or discover the art of savouring pleasure. I have met Friends who felt compelled to move house in order to escape from being over-burdened with too many Quaker offices and chores. If our present structures are so cumbersome that conscientious Friends have no time to savour and enjoy life then our recent efforts at restructuring are to be welcomed as long overdue.

I also used the T-shirt exercise that I described at the beginning of this chapter at a Day Conference with (what was then) Gloucester and Nailsworth Monthly Meeting. We spent one session looking at the ways in which the Western Churches have seen the Spirit operating almost exclusively within the Church and in strictly religious experiences like salvation and sanctification. We looked at the ways in which the spiritual life was seen as a way of detaching its practitioners from this world; and how it encouraged those who were intent on living a holy life to be deeply suspicious of pleasure, hostile to the body and to distrust almost everything to do with the natural world. We talked about 'the Ladder of Ascent or Perfection' that was once a popular symbol for would-be spiritual athletes.

At the end of the day an elderly Friend came to me grinning all over her face and said, 'You know I always thought I was not a spiritual person. And now I know that I am'. Another Friend came and said with great glee, 'I've done it. I've kicked away the ladder'. There is a real sense of release when people realise that the things that give them the greatest joy are blessings given them by a God who also relishes them and intends them, not only to be enjoyed but also to be the means by which our spirits are nourished and refreshed. Therefore they are part of our spirituality and whenever they delight and revive us we can truly say 'That's the Spirit'.

In the final part of his Swarthmore Lecture Alex Wildwood pleads for what he calls 'a passionate, juicy Quakerism' and one that refuses to tame or domesticate the Spirit. He begins by quoting the words of the Korean Feminist theologian, Chung Hyun

Kyung, who led the opening session of the World Council of Churches Assembly on the theme of 'Come Holy Spirit, Renew the whole Creation':

> I want us to echo the words of Chung Hyun Kyung, 'Let us welcome the Spirit, letting ourselves go in her wild rhythm of life', trusting our heart memory, the cellular intelligence that brought us through four and a half billion years of evolution to this moment in time. I pray for us to be passionate and unpredictable as well as prudent (which we do so well), unfettered by convention and precedent, but informed by experience, always alive to the Spirit in all, soul-full, expressive, compassionate and seeking wisdom and the truth revealed to us in the moment, respecting the God-given gift of the sensuous, understanding the erotic as life's longing for communion with itself. ... My vision is of a passionate, juicy Quakerism, of disciplined rebels and surrendered individualists, a creative order of mundane religious, a company of mutually encouraging, authentic and inspiring fools for that God who is the source of everything.[16]

What else can we learn about the Spirit that will enable us to identify it and further explore what it means to be a 'Community of the Spirit'? I think that two of the most illuminating books about the Holy Spirit that I have read are by John Taylor, who before his retirement was Bishop of Winchester. One was *The Go-between God* and the other *A Matter of Life and Death*. In the first he suggests that the Spirit is the mediator or messenger between God and human beings, but also between human beings, and between us and the rest of creation.[17]

Scientists who are busy exploring the world of quantum mechanics and the behaviour of elementary particles, tell us that when two particles are attracted to each other they cannot actually make contact with one another without a third particle, a kind of messenger particle, who goes between them and effects the introduction. In both books John Taylor suggests that this what the Holy Spirit does. He is the go-between who enables the encounter to take place.

He works this out more fully in the second of his studies on the Holy Spirit, *A Matter of Life and Death*. In the first chapter of

[16] *A faith to call our own*, pp. 97 & 99. [17] *The Go-Between God*, p. 19

the book he describes one particular experience that brought this home to him. He was returning from Oxford to London on a late summer evening, reading a paperback and glancing up from it from time to time. Suddenly he was aware, or made aware, of the landscape through which the train was passing. It was quite an ordinary one, stubble fields, corn stooks and long blue shadows from the stooks to the glowing trees beyond. He was moved by the beauty of it and found himself wondering what actually happens when a landscape, a tree, or the night sky suddenly presents itself and seems to demand attention. He observed that somehow that quite ordinary scene beyond the railway track had ceased to be just an object he was looking at.

> It had become a subject imbued with a power that was affecting me, saying something to me in the way that music does. Something had generated a current of charged intensity between it and me. ... Who effects the introduction between me and that which is there, turning it into a presence towards which I surrender myself.[18]

As soon as he had asked himself that particular question the answer came to him. 'So this is what is meant by the Holy Spirit,' and he realised that this was the work of the Spirit. He was the universal communicator 'working from within [human beings] making them more aware'.

I imagine that we have all had experiences like that when for some reason that may bear no relation to what is happening to us in our day to day life, a bit of the world, a landscape, a person or a new thought suddenly sparks into life for us and we feel that we are being addressed by something within that experience; we are quite literally 'inspired' by it. Brian Keenan, held as a hostage in Lebanon, describes the moments of vivid awareness when one of his captors brought him a bowl of fruit. He describes the bowl and its contents, some apricots, some small oranges, some nuts, cherries and a banana. And suddenly the fruits and the colours mesmerise him and send him into a quiet rapture:

> I lift an orange into the flat, filthy palm of my hand, and feel and smell and lick it. The colour orange, the colour, the colour, my God the colour orange. Before me is a feast of

---

18 *A Matter of Life and Death*, p. 3

colour. I feel myself begin to dance, slowly. I am intoxicated by colour ... Such wonder, such absolute wonder in such an insignificant fruit.[19]

He goes on to describe the experience in more detail. He is filled with a quiet joy that is somehow so complete that it is beyond the meaning of joy. The world is somehow re-created for him in that small broken bowl of fruit. 'I am drunk with something I can understand but cannot explain. I am filled with a sense of love. I am filled and satiated by it ... For days I sit in a kind of dreamy lethargy, in part contemplation, in part worship'.

Of course, it can happen in less dramatic ways, though often, I believe, when external events are difficult or painful. I remember an occasion, several years ago, when my arthritis became very much worse and for some weeks was so severe that I could hardly walk at all. And I was in a considerable amount of pain. I felt quite bleak about it. It seemed to mean the end of our walking and flower-hunting holidays in the Alps and our long walks across the Sussex downs. I was feeling very gloomy.

A friend drove us from Sussex into Hampshire, to a garden centre in the grounds of Stansted House. As soon as we got there my friends went off to look at flowers and suggested that I make my way to the tea garden and wait for them there. I hobbled off, making very slow progress and feeling very ancient. I got myself a cup of coffee and a cheese scone and went to sit in the garden. There were only a few people about just talking quietly to one another. I sat facing a wide green lawn and a gloriously colourful herbaceous border. There was no sound of traffic. It was very peaceful. And quite suddenly my depression fell away and I was completely happy, held in a very deep kind of peace. I simply sat there absorbed in the beauty of what was a fairly ordinary corner of the garden. There was nothing spectacular about it. And yet it seemed to shine with a kind of luminous glow. I was content to be there just looking and being.

John Taylor insists that all these moments of intense awareness when something shines out for us, often when we least expect it, are moments when the Spirit is acting as the go-between, opening our eyes to the wonder of the world, or the wonder of another human being, or the miracle of human creativity that has so

[19] *An Evil Cradling*, p. 68–69.

enriched our world. It is the work of the Spirit to open our eyes and make us more aware. 'The Spirit of God is at work to bring us to life, to make us more awake and aware, and so to lead us to fresh discovery and a fresh response'.[20]

George Fox was right in discerning the Spirit mightily at work among Friends, giving them new insights into the Bible, sharper eyes to the social injustice around them, and fresh light on what it means to be a community led by the Spirit. He was wrong in believing that this could only happen inside the faith community and only in the life of someone who had turned to the Light and was obedient to it. He was wrong in believing that Friends were the final expression of the Church, the only ones who were being led by the Spirit, the only ones who had got it right. He would, I think, have found it hard to understand what Alex Wildwood meant when he talked about a 'juicy' Quakerism or what I meant by my T-Shirt exercise. But then, of course, he was a child of his age, as we are of ours.

Jürgen Moltmann was concerned to rescue the word 'spirit' from its narrow religious cage because he believed that we need its cosmic meaning today as perhaps never before. In the preface to 'Spirit of Life' he observed that in our contemporary situation of planetary crisis and violent conflict and so much blighted and ruined life it is hard for us to affirm life whole-heartedly. 'So the essential thing is to affirm life – the life of other creatures – the life of other people – our own lives. ... But anyone who really says 'yes' to life says 'no' to war. Anyone who really loves life says 'no' to poverty. So the people who truly affirm and love life take up the struggle against violence and injustice. They refuse to get used to it. They do not conform. They resist'.[21] I imagine that Friends, including George Fox, would unite with that concern and say 'Yes. That's the Spirit'.

---

[20] *A Matter of Life and Death*, p. 4. [21] *The Spirit of Life*, p. xii.

Chapter 7
Universe as Revelation

Alex Wildwood

We are literally made from the products of stellar furnaces that exploded billions of years ago, explosions that seeded our section of space with the building blocks for life itself. These ideas place science and religion into uncanny and unfamiliar congruity: we have been created by forces of virtually infinite range, subtlety and power.

Douglas Watt[1]

We humans are not separate creatures on Earth, in a Universe. We are a mode of being of Earth, an expression of the Universe.

Michael Dowd[2]

Many of those who have been catapulted beyond Earth's gravitational embrace have proclaimed afterwards a common visionary experience and a greater passion for life on Earth. They have grasped experientially what Thomas Berry calls 'The Great Story' – an appreciation of the origins and unfolding of our universe as the true context of human evolution and spiritual realisation. The 'post-denominational' priest Matthew Fox pointed out that one of the unexpected consequences of the NASA space programme was that the astronauts, despite their rigorous military-scientific training, returned to Earth as mystics.

'My view of our planet was a glimpse of divinity', astronaut Edgar D. Mitchell commented, 'On the return trip homeward,

[1] 'Attachment Mechanisms and the Bridging of Science and Religion', p. 80. [2] *Thank God for Evolution*, p. 57

gazing towards the stars and the planet from which I had come, I suddenly experienced the universe as intelligent, loving, harmonious'. This experience of the awesome, mysterious integrity of our Earth from space transcended boundaries of nationality, race and religion. For the Russian cosmonaut Boris Volynov, 'Having seen the sun, the stars, and our planet, you become more full of life, softer. You begin to look at all living things with greater trepidation and you begin to be more kind and patient with the people around you'.[3]

We now understand the Universe as a 14.7 billion year continuous event (that's 14,700,000,000 years). It can be hard to grasp the vast scale of this great narrative. Taking from 'evolutionary evangelist' Michael Dowd the idea of an 'evolutionary year planner' to highlight key points on this journey, it is only in early September that our solar system appears out of an exploded supernova; dinosaurs live for a few days in early December, and the universe begins 'reflecting consciously in and through the human, with choice and free will, less than ten minutes before midnight on December 31st'.[4]

This understanding of a continuous evolutionary process can help us realise in a new way something our ancestors intuited as they told their tales and danced by firelight beneath the overarching sky. With this, and with the icon of the Earth from space, we are called to a new awareness of the holy not as something Other; that 'the whole thing is holy' and 'the conditions under which life is granted to us are graceful, are filled with grace', as Miriam MacGillis has put it.[5]

But this is not the story we have told ourselves or taught to our children. Our foundational cultural stories (from both the Judeo-Christian and Greek humanistic traditions) were shaped within what Thomas Berry calls 'the assumption of a radical discontinuity' between the human and the more-than-human world. This assumption of an absolute divide between humanity and the rest has been enshrined in both our religious and secular teachings. (Which is why Darwin's theory of evolution by natural selection, which provided the mechanism by which our kinship with the rest of biological life could be established, was so incendiary.)

3 Mitchell and Volynov quoted by Michael Dowd in *EarthSpirit*, pp. 97, 98 and 95. [4]*Ibid.*, p. 23. [5] 'The New Cosmology – its implication for our lives', see Chapter 5, note 5.

We can now appreciate that our kinship with the rest of life as it has evolved out of the Universe process is no longer simply a poetic image but a crucial fact of our existence – and this awareness is a vital aspect of the spiritual awakening that is happening at this time. The new understanding of the story of our universe has profound implications for how we view ourselves and the divine mystery at the heart of life.

We need to understand in a new way our particular responsibilities as a species, our role within the cosmic order – not from an assumption of separation and superiority but from an awareness of the interdependence of the whole; we need to embrace what Elizabeth A. Johnson and other feminists call the *kinship* paradigm:

> Human spirit expressed in self consciousness and freedom is not something new added to the universe from outside. Rather, it is a sophisticated evolutionary expression of the capacity for self-organization and creativity inherent in the universe itself.[6]

Our expanding universe, with its fifty billion galaxies, each composed of a more than a hundred billion stars, is perhaps the most wondrous process the human mind can contemplate. It has been calculated[7] that if the universe had expanded even slightly faster or slower than it did – even by as little as a trillionth of a per cent – the matter in the cosmos would have either collapsed back into a black hole or expanded so rapidly that it would have evaporated. The very fact of existence is a miracle.

'The new cosmology' arose out of two key discoveries in the early twentieth century. Through astronomical observation, it was realised that we live in an expanding universe. Our current understanding is that all the energy of our universe was present at the initial moment of its genesis – what is popularly referred to as 'the Big Bang' (although to describe it as any kind of 'Bang' is neither accurate nor poetically satisfying; Miriam MacGillis speaks of 'a radiant emergence of energy'). In that primal fireball, the original flaring forth of space and time, everything began expanding and has continued to do so ever since – scientists debate whether the universe may, in fact, fluctuate between

6 *Women, Earth & Creator Spirit*, p. 38. 7 See, for example, Paul Davies, *The Goldilocks Enigma*, or Martin Rees, *Just Six Numbers: The dark forces that shape the universe.*

expansion and contraction, but on such a vast timescale that we have only been able to observe its current expansion. So rather than a fixed, determined, once-created *thing*, the Universe we inhabit is better envisaged as a vast developmental *process*, not an entity but an event – the *story* of space/time evolving.

Seeing the universe as a developmental process, we can appreciate that – despite the almost unimaginably vast dimensions of space and time involved – the universe needs to be seen as a single functioning system. 'The Great Story' refers to seeing human, Earth, and cosmic history as one inspiring, sacred narrative.

The second key scientific insight came when scientists started to probe the sub-atomic world. They discovered that within each atom was a vast interior realm, the exploration of which has led to a new understanding of physical reality. In just the last hundred years, humanity has acquired the technical ability to look out into space and back into time, and into the very heart of matter. What has been revealed has fundamentally changed our understanding of reality and the nature of the universe we inhabit – see for instance the stunning collections of images from space and of the natural history of Earth juxtaposed with spiritual and mystical writings in *The Hand of God: thoughts and images reflecting the Spirit of the Universe*, and *Reflections on the nature of God*, edited by Michael Reagan.

Today, rather than imagining physical reality as composed of discrete packets of inert matter – mere dead 'stuff' – physicists increasingly speak of atomic particles as 'energy events'. The reductionist approach of understanding things by taking them apart or defining entities by their component parts is today complemented by a greater appreciation of systems and inter-relatedness. In the last couple of centuries we have been able to observe, through telescopes, microscopes and now the power of computers, that at every level, each whole is also part of a larger system and that at every level, each whole-part, each 'holon', expresses its own unique kind of creativity – its potential to bring something new into existence. The term 'holon' was first coined by Arthur Koestler in *The Ghost in the Machine* in 1967. A 'holon' is a system or phenomenon that is both a whole in itself as well as a part of a larger system. Since every holon (as a part) is embedded in a larger system, it both influences and is influenced by these larger wholes. Similarly, as a whole, it is both influenced by and influences its components or subsystems. Information flows in both directions to the mutual benefit of every whole/part – unless there is a breakdown in the relationship (for example when cancer cells proliferate in the body of an organism).

Using the analogy of Russian Dolls, Michael Dowd develops the idea of holons by inviting us to picture reality as a series of 'nested dolls of increasing size and complexity'.[8] So subatomic particles reside within atoms which themselves compose molecules, cells, organisms and eventually complex organisms and cultures. Dowd and his wife the science writer Connie Barlow have spent the last decade travelling around the United States exploring the implications of the Great Story with audiences in churches, colleges and community halls. He sees his ministry as exploring how a sacred understanding of natural systems can 'provide ways of thinking and talking about Ultimate Reality, or God, that religious believers and scientific sceptics can both celebrate'. Scientific knowledge provides what he calls 'public revelation' while evolutionary spirituality needs to be grounded in 'a rationally sound, mainstream scientific understanding of the Universe.'

In his book *Thank God for Evolution*, Dowd begins the chapter 'What do we mean by "God"?' with the question: 'Do you believe in life?' Clearly, this is an absurd question. Life just is; it's a given, we're part of it whether we *believe* in it or not. But what we say *about* life, about its nature and essence, about the purposes and meaning we attach to it, is another story. The reality is indisputable, the *interpretations* are infinite. That's the way God needs to be understood in the light of the Great Story. Just as we cannot deny that there is such a thing as 'Reality as a whole' so too, Dowd suggests, 'God' is 'a legitimate, though not a required, proper name for this Ultimacy'.[9]

'Belief in God' is not the issue. 'Any "God" that can be believed in or not believed in is a trivialised notion of the divine'. In Dowd's Russian Doll analogy, God becomes 'a legitimate proper name for the largest nesting doll: the One and Only Creative Reality that is not a subset of some larger, more com-

[8] For more about Dowd's work see www.thankgodforevolution.com
[9] *Thank God for Evolution* p. 120

prehensive reality. God is that which sources and infuses everything, yet is also co-emergent with and indistinguishable from
everything'.[10]

Our understanding of the subatomic realm challenges previous ideas of matter as lifeless and inert, and this necessarily
stimulates new religious awareness: matter is not inert but, as
Elizabeth A. Johnson describes it, 'composed of atoms that are
themselves energy events ... Made up of dancing particles that
are internally constituted by their relationships, matter itself is
profoundly social ... Matter, alive with energy, evolves to spirit'.[11]

Increasingly, scientists are discovering the mysteriousness
of matter itself at the subatomic level, coining phrases such as
'Quantum weirdness' to describe what they observe.[12] In his
book *The Hidden Heart of the Cosmos: Humanity & the New Story*,
mathematical physicist Brian Swimme responds to the question
'Where does the Universe Come from?' He invites us to imagine
holding an enclosed space of air in our hands and how, if we
took away all the atoms, all the small particles, the neutrinos, all
the radiation energy in the form of invisible light, all the photons
from the original flaring-forth of the universe, we would be left
with what physicists define as a 'vacuum', 'emptiness' or 'pure
space'. What's extraordinary, he says, is that 'Even where there
are no atoms, and no elementary particles, and no protons, and
no photons, suddenly elementary particles will emerge. The particles simply foam into existence'.[13] He calls this 'an empty full-
ness, a fecund nothingness' in which 'The base of the universe
seethes with creativity, so much so that physicists refer to the universe's ground state as "space-time foam".'[14]

Space itself can no longer be considered as simply an emptiness waiting to be filled, but rather as what Duane Elgin elegantly calls 'a dynamically constructed transparency'. We are
offered today, he argues, the revelatory insight that 'the entire
cosmos is being regenerated at each instant in a single symphony
of expression that unfolds from the most minute aspects of the
subatomic realm to the vast reaches of thousands of billions of

10 *Thank God for Evolution*, p. 119, 120. 11 *Women, Earth, and Creator
Spirit*, p. 36–7. 12 See: 'Quantum weirdness: what we call reality is just
a state of mind', Bernard d'Espagnat, www.guardian.co.uk/science/
blog/2009/mar/17/templeton-quantum-entanglement
13 *The Hidden Heart of the Cosmos*, p. 92. 14 *Ibid.*, p. 93.

galactic systems'.[15] Such insights take scientists themselves into a more poetic realm of expression; the mathematician Norbert Wiener wrote: 'We are not stuff that abides, but patterns that perpetuate themselves; whirlpools of water in an ever-flowing river'.[16]

All these authors – scientists and theologians alike – point to an understanding of human intelligence and creativity as emergent properties of the Universe-process itself; we are the cosmic event coming into a self-reflexive form of consciousness. Teilhard de Chardin observed in the mid-twentieth century 'The consciousness of each of us is evolution looking at itself and reflecting upon itself'.[17]

As we seek meaningful imagery for the divine mystery today, as our sense of faith itself changes in the light of new awareness, we will need to be creative in our theologies so that they can incorporate contemporary scientific insights. In 1927, Werner Heisenberg published his now famous 'uncertainty principle' – in which he demonstrated how, even at the subatomic level, in seeking to measure or observe reality we necessarily interact with the whole in a way that affects what we observe. We are part of one universal system and we cannot observe reality 'from outside', from a supposedly disinterested, 'objective' or neutral position. We are literally one with all existence and no part of our universe can be truly understood except in its relationship to the whole. The renowned systems thinker Gregory Bateson pointed out in 1972 that 'The unit of survival is organism plus environment. We are learning by bitter experience that the organism which destroys its environment destroys itself'.[18] Each holon, each whole/part is in creative, symbiotic relationship with every other.

What the new science-based picture of reality invites us to realise is that the universe process, its entire developmental unfolding, is, in Thomas Berry's phrase, a *participatory event*. This has vital implications for how we view our human role in its continuing evolution. These new discoveries from science challenge us to evolve beyond outmoded dominion and even stewardship models (assuming as they do a separation – and superiority – of

---

[15] *Promise Ahead*, p. 50. [16] Quoted in Elgin, *Promise Ahead*, pp. 48–51
[17] *The Phenomenon of Man*, p. 221. [18] *Steps to an ecology of mind*, p. 491

the human from the rest). A participatory view invites us to consider our true calling, exactly what we humans bring to the feast.

We are 'a means by which Nature can appreciate its beauty and feel its splendour' (Michael Dowd);[19] we are 'the cantors of the universe', (Elizabeth Johnson).[20] One of the wonderful things about the Great Story is that it is 'a creation story that is not over yet'[21] – we can expect that our understanding will evolve. But at present we can conjecture that humanity is that part of the universe process able to reflect on this Great Story and celebrate it – but not as an impartial, 'objective' observer, not as the 'crown of creation', separate and aloof from everything else. We are now invited to see ourselves as one cell in a greater body – albeit a cell that has the capacity to observe and sense something of the awesome mystery of the whole. (We are also an unusual 'cell' in having the capacity to destabilise the whole system.) The paradox is that we are special not in the sense of being above or separate from the rest but because we bear a particular responsibility, a capacity for empathy with the whole; we are what Matthew Fox called 'co-creators', able to consciously work with the evolutionary impulse at the heart of the Universe.

Our inklings of the vastness of the cosmos and the intricacy of its innermost structures – which, as Job was so forcefully reminded, we did nothing to create – must surely amplify, not diminish our sense of divine presence. I'm grateful for David Cadman's proposition that 'when we speak of Divine, we cannot say "the Divine" as Divine is not a noun, cannot be turned into an object or person. Indeed, as soon as we begin to limit and shape Divine, we begin to lose divine presence'.[22] We know we are in an expanding universe, 'still in the process of becoming', in the words of Miriam MacGillis, the awesome majesty of which 'does not contain the whole of the mystery out of which it comes'.[23]

The scientific discoveries of the last century offer us fresh ways to imagine and speak of this mystery. Because in quantum physics subatomic entities can behave either as particles (with a precise location in space) or as waves (diffuse and flowing), we have the

[19] *Thank God for Evolution*, p. 57. [20] *EarthLight* magazine, vol 25, Spring 1997. [21] Connie Barlow, www.thegreatstory.org
[22] 'Enfolded in every moment', *The Friends' Quarterly*, 2001 issue 3, p. 41. [23] 'The New Cosmology – its implication for our lives', see Chapter 5, note 5.

opportunity to deal with some theological problems, imagining God as 'the living awareness in the space between the atoms' as proposed by Tom Mahon (author of ebooks mainly for children, such as *A History of the Universe by Edward: The oldest electron there ever was*): 'Is God immanent or transcendent, internal or external, composed or compassionate? Like the question of whether the atom is wave or particle, the answer is yes'.[24]

Of course, to imagine divine presence in new ways – such as 'a holy name for Ultimate Reality', 'the all-encompassing Wholeness'[25] – begs a number of important questions. Does this 'God' evoke a sense of humility, love, trust, reverence, or devotion? Is this a 'God' we might worship or pray to? Is this a picture of God that inspires us to service, compassion and generosity? What does faithfulness look like with this new understanding of divine presence?

These are questions I ask myself on a regular basis. When Tim Peat Ashworth and I were travelling to Quaker meetings around the country I was once accused of a kind of 'neo-Buddhism' in my non-theistic presentation – and it's true, there are days when the idea of a God 'out there' makes no sense to me. But at other times (and first thing when I wake in the morning) I find myself wanting to be thankful for another instalment in the gracious gift of life; I understand the desire to give thanks to something more personal than 'the mysterious creative power at the heart of the universe-process'! Sometimes I pray using the words 'Originating/Creative Mystery'; on other occasions I find myself using the Jewish term 'Holy One'; I like the ambiguity of the latter, both real and relational in a personal way yet referring to the mystery of the Whole, beyond any name or comprehension. I also find in prayer I use terms like 'Source of All' or 'Great Mystery', which my Buddhist-leaning self is satisfied may be simply consciousness itself, or it may be love; it remains ineffable. Yet by using such terms I invoke a quality of intimacy and tenderness in the relationship and, crucially, I acknowledge my small self's dependence on this mysterious birthing power at the heart of all things.

Michael Dowd suggests the term 'creatheism' to embrace both the atheist affirmation 'that all language of Ultimate Reality,

---

[24] Quoted in *Reflections on the nature of God* ed. Michael Reagan, p. 44.
[25] *Thank God for Evolution*, p. 131

without exception, is metaphorical (i.e. there is not an invisible being up there somewhere)' but also to realise that if we are going to relate to Reality personally, 'it is both acceptable and beneficial to use metaphors to engage the heart – metaphors such as Father, Mother, Beloved, Larger Self, Higher Power ...'[26]

While we need to accept that all our images of God are limited, for me 'humanist' or 'atheist' Quakers miss the point. Just because all our images of God are inevitably human constructs it does not follow that there is no reality in what our (necessarily limited) symbols point to. In asserting the non-reality of God (often evangelically) such non-theist Friends miss out on the creative challenge of expressing our collective religious experience of 'God' in new metaphors and symbols. Maybe talking about 'relating to Reality as a whole' may become a language we can share as Friends today.

The Great Story challenges us to articulate our experience of the numinous in a new way. For me it is a satisfying attempt to reconcile the facts of our cosmic evolution with the human need for a mythic narrative, something more poetic and inspiring than facts alone. The Great Story also provides a factual grounding, a counterbalance to the tendency of contemporary expressions of spirituality to be 'airy-fairy' and excessively subjective; the science of it is satisfying to the mind while the story itself invokes the sense of awe and wonder that are at the heart of the religious impulse. But for the story to really come alive for us we need to explore it through art and ritual, we need to feel it in our bodies as well understanding it with our minds. Around the world people are doing just that – creating new forms of ritual that can help us to experience the story of our planet and its embeddedness in the Universe. One way to do this is the practice (originally devised by Miriam MacGillis) called 'The Cosmic Walk' (an impression of which is given in the Appendix).[27]

But how do we develop a meaningful relationship to the Whole of Reality? Traditional spiritual disciplines and modern psychology alike both suggest that the path to wholeness – or right relationship to Reality, or spiritual awakening – has certain

26 *Thank God for Evolution*, p. 130.
27 www.threeeysofuniverse.org gives details of versions of the ritual form devised by Miriam McGillis; see also *Walking the Sacred Story* by Erna & Michael Colebrook.

common features. Michael Dowd suggests how we might think in terms of a synthesis of these disciplines, ancient and modern, in this time:

> The peace that passes all understanding, recovery from addiction, salvation from sin, ongoing transformation, personal empowerment, enlightenment, dwelling in the kingdom of heaven, experiencing oneness with God – each of these can be found right here, now (and nowhere else!) How? Simply, get that you are part of the Whole, live with integrity, express your creativity, take responsibility for your life and your evolutionary legacy, listen from your heart to discern guidance from the source of your existence (whatever you may choose to call It/Him/Her), and love the Whole of Reality with all your heart, mind, soul, and strength, and your neighbour as yourself.[28]

As spiritual seekers in a time of transition, when we can no longer assume to share a common religious idiom, we need to ask ourselves, 'What story inspires me to loving service? What story helps me transcend self-centredness and the constraints of what mystic Eckhart Tolle calls "the egoic mind"?' Personally I do find such inspiration in this new story of our origins, in this profound sense of our interconnectedness, that 'We are each completely unique yet completely connected with the entire universe' (Duane Elgin).[29]

There is an ethic that flows from realising our relatedness to all that exists – and it turns out to be, not surprisingly, remarkably similar to that of traditional religion at its best. The meaning and purpose of our lives is to be found in how we contribute to the wellbeing of others; the purpose of humanity as a whole can be measured by how much we collectively contribute to the larger body of Life. (At the moment we're not doing very well.) Really taking on board how life has emerged on Earth, how our solar system was birthed from dying stars, we more deeply appreciate that human destiny and the destiny of the Earth are completely interlinked. Our destiny, our purpose in the context of this cosmic story is to further evolutionary creativity in ways that

---

[28] Dowd, Seattle address, 2002; see also *Thank God for Evolution*, pp. 123–24 on 'the path to wholeness and right relationship to Reality'.
[29] *Promise Ahead*, p. 66–67

are life-giving for the whole.

The real miracle of creation for Thomas Berry is that the Divine, 'in creating the universe makes a universe that creates itself'.[30] 'God' we can accept is a valid, if not obligatory, name for what Michael Dowd describes as 'the inner dynamic guiding the process, the living reality revealed in and through creation'.[31] The new cosmology – with its view of the universe as a single, living entity – invites us to see freedom, spontaneous creativity and uncertainty as emergent properties at the heart of the Universe process. With absolutely everything connected to everything else in one vast interacting Whole, creativity is at the core of every aspect of it: Duane Elgin quotes the physicist Freeman Dyson saying that in quantum mechanics, matter is 'an active agent, constantly making choices between alternative possibilities … It appears that mind, as manifested by the capacity to make choices, is to some extent inherent in every electron'. Elgin points out that this is not to suggest that all consciousness is of the same kind, but that even an atom 'has a reflective capacity appropriate to its form and function'.[32]

In his book *Promise Ahead: A vision of hope and action for humanity's future*, Duane Elgin compares our emerging scientific understanding of the creative, participatory nature of reality with the worldview of some of the traditional, Earth-centred cultures of the world. He cites Luther Standing Bear, a Lakota elder: 'Everywhere there was life, visible and invisible, and every object gave us a great interest in life. The world teemed with life and wisdom; there was no complete solitude for the Lakota'. Elgin summarises this worldview: 'For the Lakota … religion was based on a direct experience of an all-pervading spirit throughout the world. Since a life-force was felt to be in and through everything, all things were seen as being connected and related. Because everything is an expression of the Great Spirit, everything deserves to be treated with respect'.[33]

I remember how as an undergraduate I wanted to learn all about these primal peoples. In large part this was because I sensed that they did not share our cultural alienation, our painful, self-imposed exile from the Earth and from the rest of life.

30 *The Great Story* (video). 31 *EarthSpirit*, p. 18. 32 Freeman Dyson, *Infinite in all directions*, quoted in *Promise Ahead*, p. 53.
33 *Promise Ahead*, p. 64–65

While undoubtedly I had a romanticised vision of such tribal cultures, it is clearly one of the tragedies of our age that the rapacious appetite of our globalised industrial growth society is fast destroying the last remnants of such peoples and their way of life, obliterating the precious resource of these ancient traditions, these memory-cells of human ingenuity and sustainable, Earth-centred coexistence. Decimated by mercenaries in the pay of 'developers', vulnerable to infection from contact with outsiders, deprived of their traditional lands and nomadic way of life, primal peoples have been pushed to the margins of our world. (For further information see Survival International;[34] for a sobering perspective on our life-denying civilisation and the suppression of wildness in the Western psyche, see Derrick Jensen, *A Language Older Than Words*, and Jerry Mander, *In the Absence of the Sacred*.)

I remember some years ago walking around in the Van Gogh museum in Amsterdam, and at one point I suddenly felt simply overwhelmed; I found a quiet corner where I could sit as I suddenly found myself moved to tears. I experienced a vibrancy, an ineffable spirit of the artist himself in the original paintings, completely lacking from the reproductions I had known. In some mysterious way I felt connected with his perception of reality as I came in close proximity to his actual brush marks, the texture and placing of the paint upon the canvas.

Something about Van Gogh has always touched me deeply in ways I didn't understand; not just his tragic suicide but something about the way he saw the world. Reading Elgin's book I suddenly made sense of the grief I felt that day in Amsterdam. Describing the worldview of the Native American Ohlones (the first human inhabitants of what is now Silicon Valley in California) Elgin quotes anthropologist Malcolm Margolin:

> The Ohlones, then, lived in a world perhaps somewhat like a Van Gogh painting, shimmering and alive with movement and energy in ever-changing patterns. It was a world in which thousands of living, feeling, magical things, all operating on dream-logic, carried out their individual actions ... Power was everywhere, in everything, and therefore every act was religious.[35]

[34] www.survival-international.org

[35] Malcolm Margolin, *The Ohlone Way*, quoted in *Promise Ahead*, p. 65.

Suddenly, I realised why Van Gogh's paintings spoke to me so deeply; they touched my heartfelt yearning for another way of seeing and being present in the world. Through his costly fidelity to his own sense of reality, Vincent Van Gogh touched a hidden longing buried deep within me, a desire for an intimacy with the world of energetic form.

In that moment I sensed the Light within in a new way – not exactly as our Quaker forebears witnessed to it, as a seed of divine consciousness, something of the wholly Other, graciously planted within our human hearts: rather, I sensed it as both a truly Inner as well as Inward Light, as the shimmering movement and energy of existence itself, present throughout the universe, which we can sense, can 'listen' to when we still our busy minds, when we sink down beneath the ego's illusion of separateness into the well of consciousness itself and touch the *anima mundi*, the soul of the world. In Van Gogh's paintings I felt what Elgin calls 'the aliveness that is at the foundation of the universe'. Sensing my own small life nested like a Russian doll within the matrix of all life and all existence, I find in Elgin's words a profound expression of faith: '… we are not disconnected from the larger universe, and never have been'.[36]

Experiencing reality as inherently *relational*, we can see ourselves, not as the products of blind chance created by indifferent forces in a lifeless universe with no inherent sense of meaning or purpose – as Westerners have done, by and large, since the Enlightenment and more so since 'the death of God' in the nineteenth and twentieth centuries. Rather, we can sense ourselves today as the progeny, literally the offspring of what Elgin calls 'a deep-design intelligence that infuses the entire cosmos'.[37] In this new way of seeing ourselves – as an expression of a creativity inherent in the Universe process itself – we can get beyond the theists' Supreme Being, the wholly-Other God of the Creationists, and the cold, dead directionless evolution of the scientific materialists. We can rediscover the sacredness of the Whole; we can realise, as Thomas Berry so elegantly observed: 'Evolution is neither random nor determined, but creative'.[38]

Our grief at our destruction of the more-than-human world

36 Promise Ahead, p. 65. 37 *Ibid.*, p. 67. 38 Quoted in Dowd's Seattle address; see Thomas Berry, *The Great Work* p. 169ff.

may be the catalyst that moves us from our existential isolation to an experience of intimate communion with the Greater Reality of which we are a part, as we sense our human odyssey as 'a sacred journey through a living and unified cosmos'.[39]

Rather than living in fear of the old hierarchical God of divine judgement, the living universe paradigm offers us a new basis for human ethics, one based on recognition of our greater identity and on the experience of deep time. Marvelling at the increasing complexity and wondrous diversity of our interconnected world – and the evidence we find there of greater and greater differentiation, increased subjectivity, and deeper kinds of communion with itself over time – gives us a scientifically accurate understanding of how reality works but also the basis of a truly universal sacred narrative, a global basis for human ethics, irrespective of 'belief'. Such a basis for defining ethical behaviour was first championed in the modern age by Aldo Leopold in 1948 when he proposed his now-famous 'land ethic': 'A thing is right when it tends to preserve the integrity, stability, and beauty of the biotic community. It is wrong when it tends otherwise'.[40] In terms of the Great Story we can define 'good' (ethical, moral) behaviour as that which preserves or benefits, over time, the related larger holons of our existence, while 'bad' (immoral, unethical) behaviour is that which, over time, harms or diminishes the larger and/or smaller holons of our existence.

All this may seem a long way from our traditional Quaker understandings of worship and witness, our understanding of prayerful discernment as 'seeking the will of God'. But in Duane Elgin's exploration of this new paradigm, he wrote something which, for me, makes sense of meeting for worship in terms of the new understanding of God/Reality I have been exploring in these pages:

> An underlying field of consciousness weaves humanity together, making it possible for us to understand intuitively what is healthy and what is not, what works and what doesn't. We can each tune into this living field and sense what is in harmony with the well-being of the whole.[41]

[39] *Promise Ahead*, p. 68.   [40] *A Sand County Almanac*, p. 89.
[41] *Promise Ahead*, p. 69.

Today, many British Friends have difficulty with the theological assumptions implicit in our description of the purpose of our business meetings as 'seeking the will of God'. I remember in a Yearly Meeting session a number of years ago, Val Ferguson spoke to this Quaker phrase, saying how for her it referred more to sensing the *direction* in which we feel we are being led; she spoke of finding a solution that was *pleasing to God* – doubtless one of many ways we might go – rather than the idea that God has a fixed will, a single right answer that in the silence and our spoken contributions we hope to have revealed to us.

Although Elgin uses very different language to early Friends, I can certainly make sense of my own Quaker experience from his account of what happens when we move beyond our small, individual sense of self – as can happen in a gathered meeting: 'When we are in alignment, we experience – as a sort of kinaesthetic sense – a positive hum of well-being'.[42] When we begin to realise the seamless fabric of creation it can awaken in us a profound sense of connection with, and compassion for, the rest of life. Our sense of empathy and concern expands as we realise the Oneness of all that exists.

We need an inspiring, credible story to live by; we need a story that explains the world we live in; we need a mythic tale that does not fly in the face of reason, which both ennobles us and keeps us humble: after all, 'without a big picture, we are very small people'.[43] We need to ground ourselves in this new scientific understanding of reality as we face an uncertain future. Brian Swimme, Director of the Center for the Story of the Universe, expresses it as:

When we see ourselves within the Universe
We will have the strength to bear
The destruction of the moment.

Only the Universe
Is large enough to bear
The suffering of the Earth.[44]

---

42 *Promise Ahead*, p. 69. 43 Joel Primack and Nancy Ellen Abrams, *The View from the Centre of the universe*. p. 84. 44 *Canticle to the Cosmos* (DVD) study guide, p. 71

Chapter 8
A God Who Stands Back
Darkness and the Absence of God

Jo Farrow

Human beings will never grow up unless we have a God who
stands back.

Jocelyn Burnell[1]

God would have us know that we must live as those who
manage our lives without God. The God who is with us is the
God who forsakes us.

Dietrich Bonhoeffer[2]

It could be that God has not absconded but spread, as our
vision and understanding of the universe have spread, to a
fabric of spirit and sense so grand and subtle, so powerful in
a new way, that we can only feel blindly of its hem.

Annie Dillard[3]

In *The World in my Heart* I wrote about my sense of 'a holy presence that has played hide and seek with me in all my journeying'.[4] Today I am more often aware of a holy absence, or, perhaps
more accurately, a God whose presence has spread to be something
woven mysteriously into the warp and weft of the universe itself.

When I first came among Friends I heaved a sigh of relief
that I no longer had to listen Sunday after Sunday to a lection-
ary of readings drawn from a Bible, written by men, mainly from

[1] Interviewed by Alison Leonard, *Living in Godless Times*, p. 33.
[2] *Letters and Papers from Prison*, p. 164. [3] *Pilgrim at Tinker Creek*, p. 20
[4] *The World in my Heart*, p. 16

the point of view of male patriarchal understanding of God. I no longer had to bewail and bemoan my sins and confess them to a critical-parent Judge and invoke the death of His Son in order to wipe the slate clean. I no longer had to listen to sermons expounding a male perception of Biblical texts. Nor did I have to sing martial hymns portraying the Christian life as military combat, or hymns of praise to an omnipotent God who, apparently, required our endless adulation. This male God was generally portrayed in those hymns as the Cosmic Super-Boss who needed, not only our continual praise, but also our unquestioning obedience to His Will. I was now in a space in which contemplative silence was of paramount importance and in which women were free to minister and hold any office. It seemed as though I had come into a community of the Spirit that was free of all those heavy patriarchal overtones.

After a while, of course, I realised how naïve I had been in assuming that Quaker Meetings are a spiritual zone uncontaminated by male theologies and male versions of spirituality. I became aware that I was still in a milieu in which all the old monarchical models of God were in the ascendant. Perhaps it was not altogether surprising. Sallie McFague[5] has observed that the monarchical model of God as divine, all powerful King with human beings his subjects, who in turn offer him loyal obedience, is one of the oldest models and still the most prevalent. As Rosemary Radford Ruether has reminded us, 'Male monotheism has been so taken for granted in Judeo-Christian culture that the peculiarity of imaging God solely through one gender has not been recognized'.[6]

Emphasis on God's omnipotence and absolute sovereignty were characteristics of Calvinistic and Lutheran models of the divine. It was certainly the model that dominated George Fox's spirituality and it has played a major part in the construction of Quaker life and thought. We insist that in our meetings for worship and for church affairs our aim is to discern and be obedient to the will of God. We continue, apparently, to view God as a supreme being who commands our unquestioning obedience in spite of the fact that this is not a way of defining the divine that would make much sense in our contemporary understanding of

[5] *Models of God*, pp. 63–69. [6] *Sexism and God Talk*, p. 53

loving parental relationships.

Anne Primavesi argues that this view of God stemmed from conventional interpretations of the Genesis creation stories. 'When it came to interpreting the Genesis narrative, there were no competing stories to place against that of God as a despotic parent who demanded under pain of death total obedience from the creatures of a world under his power'.[7] She points out that Augustine's interpretation of the Genesis stories sprang from the context of a hierarchical Roman society in which emperors exercised total control over their subjects, land owners could exploit and flog the peasants who worked for them and male heads of households had absolute authority over wives, children and slaves. Unfortunately Augustine's understanding of God's authority over human beings became the standard Christian view.

We may need to ask ourselves some questions about whether our experience in Quaker meetings supports this view of being divinely directed by a 'God who has a right to demand our obedience', and to ask ourselves whether, in fact, the idea of being *told what to do* is consistent with the image of a nurturing God who, presumably, wants us to grow up and become spiritually mature. We have been given intelligence; imagination, enquiring and creative minds and presumably any God who endowed us with such gifts would want us to use them in our decision-making and in our vocal ministry.

It is feminist theologians like Sallie McFague who have helped us to see that the monarchical model is a dangerous one. It locates God as external to the world. It assumes that all power and goodness are in this almighty Being and that human beings are as nothing unless they are obedient to His Will. Janet Scott, in her Swarthmore Lecture, also observes that there are real difficulties with metaphors that focus on the kingship and transcendence of God.[8]

In the 2005 Swarthmore Lecture, Helen Steven reflects on the fact that John Robinson's runaway best seller *Honest to God*, and the writings of Teilhard de Chardin and Paul Tillich, all influenced the way in which our generation thought about God, and called into question 'the whole concept of an all-powerful

[7] *Making God Laugh*, p. 92. [8] *What Canst Thou Say?*, p. 77

father figure, dwelling in a far-off heaven, able to dispense justice and intervene dramatically in the affairs of human life'.[9] She goes on to admit, as Sally McFague has done, that this idea of an all-powerful, transcendent God is deeply rooted in our culture, and observes 'how embedded in our psyche is the idea of a male, dominant and often vengeful God'.

Throughout this book we have written about 'the death of theism'; but it is important to remember that the death of traditional ways of thinking about God does not mean the death of God. It may be that it does for some people. But it doesn't for me, and it doesn't for John Shelby Spong, who writes that although there is something lonely and frightening about accepting that we are not spiritual toddlers dependent on a parent God, if we can move beyond our anxiety and are able to confront the new reality we may discover that there is actually something invigorating about finding a new maturity and discovering that we can approach God in a radically different way. He speaks of his awareness of God, rather as Tillich did, as the 'Ground and Source of All Being'.[10]

In this liminal time of living 'between stories' there is, for some of us, a real awareness of absence and loss, of experiencing the darkness of the numinous Mystery we have named as God. And this is difficult for us when the traditional understanding of our meetings for worship seem to enshrine a quite different view of God.

Thomas Kelly, in his reflections on the gathered meeting, writes: 'What is the ground and foundation of the gathered meeting? In the last analysis, it is, I am convinced, the Real Presence of God'.[11] This has been for the past three hundred and fifty years the Quaker interpretation of the basis of our meetings for worship. Our 'Advices and Queries' contain references to our awareness of the presence of God. Devotional books, including Brother Lawrence's classic *The Practice of the Presence of God*, make continual reference to this sense of 'the presence', and assume that it is the aim of our spiritual practices. But I find myself coming back again and again to Jocelyn Burnell's 'Human beings will never grow up unless we have a God who stands back'.[12]

[9] *No Extraordinary Power*, pp. 71–72. [10] *A New Christianity for a New World*, pp. 59–60. [11] *Quaker Faith and Practice* 2.40. [12] Interviewed by Alison Leonard in *Living in Godless Times*, p. 33.

In his book of reflections on the meaning of the Resurrection, David Runcorn observes, 'The first experience of resurrection for the disciples was not presence but absence'.[13] He goes on to reflect on how strange it was that the resurrection appearances of Jesus (however we may understand the myth) were so few and far between. At such a critical time of preparation for a new age, a new kind of community of faith very different from anything the first friends of Jesus had known, we might have expected that the weeks following the resurrection event would be a time of intense training and teach-ins. 'Instead all we have is a handful of unpredictable and enigmatic encounters with individuals or groups of disciples'.[14] He goes on to point out that while endless sermons and books are written on the resurrection *presence* of Jesus his risen *absence* is almost totally ignored.

David Runcorn then goes on to suggest that this is a basic problem for people of faith. He observes that very little Christian thought has any positive understanding of the experience of the absence of God. At this point, he suggests, we tend to think that if we haven't any awareness of God's presence it must be our fault, something lacking in us.

I often wonder what newcomers to Quaker worship feel if they sit there Sunday after Sunday waiting to be aware of the presence of God, wondering what to expect, wondering if everyone else is having the experience that they are somehow missing. I appreciated the honesty of Jocelyn Burnell's response to the question as to whether she had a sense of God's presence, of God being with her. She replied that although she knew that some Friends were aware of this, she had no such sense, though she was conscious of some situations being holy situations and she looked for the spiritual in everything.

David Runcorn writes about a time of personal crisis in his own life when he came close to breakdown. He felt like giving up his work and his faith. Friends supported him and he was grateful for their concern. Often they would pray for him that God's presence should be real to him. He goes on to say that he found it impossible to tell them that it was actually the last thing that he wanted. He felt that presence as something suffocating. He wanted God's absence. He needed to know the Hebrew awareness of God that I referred to in Chapter 6, 'That's the Spirit' – as the one who gives us space.

---

13 *Rumours of Life*, p. 18.   14 *Ibid.*, p. 19.

He writes of another time when he met a friend coming out of a Christian bookshop with an armful of books with titles like *Restoring your Spiritual Passion* and *Victorious Christian Living*. As they talked together it became clear to him that his friend was in turmoil. A previously lively faith had gone totally dry on him. The books were part of his desperate attempt to revive the experience of God's presence. But God seemed distant, absent where he had once been present. Runcorn suggests that the grace God was giving him was his absence ... 'He must learn to wait in the dark and emptiness. Part of his pain was that nothing in his Christian life had prepared him for an absence of God that wasn't either the failure of faith or the death of it'.[15] It seems, then, that for some people of faith it is a relief and a release to be aware of a God who withdraws to allow us space. But for others the idea or the experience of God's absence is a devastating one.

By contrast, the Eastern Orthodox Church has always understood the importance of the divine absence. In a way that is strikingly absent in the Western Churches, the Orthodox tradition has also always taught the importance of darkness, the desert, and spiritual emptiness in the experience of the faithful. The very first chapter in Anthony Bloom's *School for Prayer* is on 'The Absence of God'. In an interview with Timothy Wilson, Bloom (then Metropolitan Anthony of Sourozh) says 'We must be prepared for a period when God is not there for us and we must be aware of not trying to substitute a false God ... The day when God is absent, when he is silent – that is the beginning of prayer'.[16]

Quakers have emphasised their belief that in meeting for worship Christ is there, 'the Presence in the Midst'. Like other Churches in the Western tradition we have neglected to talk about the experience of God's absence. We have over-emphasised the themes of being 'in the Light', 'waiting in the Light' and 'walking in the Light' and failed to say anything about waiting and walking in the dark, though in practice that is the real test of faith, as well as an essential part of the experience of mystics in the apophatic tradition. It is salutary for us as Quakers to find Matthew Fox writing: 'A light-oriented spirituality is superficial, surface-like, lacking as it does the deep, dark roots that nourish and surprise and ground the large tree'.[17]

[15] *Rumours of Life*, p. 20.   [16] *The Essence of Prayer*, p. xix.
[17] *Original Blessing*, p. 135.

So many of the really important things go on in the dark, Matthew Fox has noticed: the internal mystery of the working of our bodies, the first nine months of our lives, and our conception, the seed growing under the ground. In a later book with Rupert Sheldrake, he reflects on the discovery by physicists that 'The whole of the Universe or ninety per cent of it is dark mystery' and on the fact that 'This is the via negativa theme of the mystics, that illumination comes at the end of the bottoming out in the darkness experience'.[18] In the same book Rupert Sheldrake points out that light is impossible unless there is also darkness. One example of this is the eye itself. The centre of the pupil is black and that is because the inside of the eye is black. We can only see light because that which receives it is dark. He goes on to point out that, paradoxically; darkness is contained within light itself, as experiments with diffraction have demonstrated.

Matthew Fox goes on to explore what it means to let go of all images, since images imply light. We only see images in the light. He observes that, as some mystics have suggested: 'One method and one path into spiritual depth is to let go of all images, even our most cherished ones, including all visual images and audio images and to sink into the silence'.[19] In Path ll in *Original Blessing* in which he is exploring ways of 'befriending the darkness' and 'letting go', he suggests that there are a number of ways of going into the deepest silence. For some it may be just sitting, for others the moments after an ecstatic experience in nature or music, or lovemaking. But he concludes with the suggestion that meditation in a Quaker meeting 'is a fine occasion for such letting go'.[20] He repeats this in his dialogue on 'darkness' with Rupert Sheldrake: 'I want to think of darkness as not just visual darkness but audio darkness, silence. For that kind of darkness I would propose that Quakers have probably done the best job in the West of late. They honour silence and are present to silence'.[21]

In contemporary astronomy black holes are mysterious reservoirs of energy. In fact they are not really black at all. They are white hot. It has been estimated that one black hole could run ten large power stations. They represent the final collapse of a

[18] *Natural Grace*, pp. 120–21. [19] *Ibid.*, pp. 122. [20] *Original Blessing* p. 138. [21] *Natural Grace*, p. 137

star into a form of pure energy. In cosmic terms they are like the emptiness and darkness that mystics have described as the *via negativa* or the apophatic way. But as Alex mentions in the previous chapter, in quantum terms empty space is never really empty. It is always active and teeming with energy. Recent research suggests that black holes are not as destructive as earlier research assumed. In fact, as Diarmuid O' Murchu observes, 'evidence to the contrary is accumulating, suggesting that they may be reservoirs of enormously creative energy giving birth to galaxies, planets, and even to creatures like ourselves'.[22] In other words they offer us a cosmic clue that the heart of darkness is the crucible of creativity and new life.

All the mystical traditions affirm that there is something deep and important to be learned by daring to make the journey into darkness. Alan Jones in his book 'Soul Making' writes: 'We long to be free; but often the kind of freedom we want is to be free of responsibility, creativity and maturity. We want to go back, to regress; we want to turn away from the kind of freedom that may be summoning us into a "Darkness" in which our true liberty may be found'.[23] We are back again at the point where God, as it were, stands back, in order for us to grow up and learn to stand on our own feet.

I can still remember sitting in the Cadbury Room at Woodbrooke during the follow-up to the International Theological Conference for Quaker women, listening to an address by Zoë White on 'Living Faithfully with Passion'. It was she who introduced me to Alan Jones' book, which is a study of the Desert Way of spirituality. In her address she talked about the need to be willing 'to enter the desert – to feel deserted by the known, and to face a fearful intimacy with the unknown … We have to face the terrors that are within, if we are to find the courage and spiritual authority to confront the tyrannies without'.[24] She spoke about her debt to those within the Judaic-Christian Tradition who had dared to become outsiders, those who had dared to stand at the very edge of the tradition, refusing the conventional or safe ways of being part of it. She was in effect talking about the need to go into the darkness in which God seems absent, in which he

22 *Quantum Theology*, p. 134. 23 *Soul Making*, p. 111.
24 *Living Faithfully with Passion*, p. 11.

withdraws in order to allow us to become more mature and independent beings.

I owe a debt of gratitude to Zoë White for reminding me of things I had known, and forgotten that I knew; for enabling me to understand that being deserted by the known is a real but necessary bereavement. The things we once knew, or thought we knew, are stripped away from us so that we are empty enough for the new to find a place in us. In a way she helped me to trust the wildness in myself again. I can remember thinking, with a rush of recognition – 'Yes, I have always been, in some way or other, a Desert person'. I was very surprised at that, because I am not a very bold or adventurous person, but I did recognise something in myself that was trekking away from the known, and I realised that I did know something about what she calls 'a fearful intimacy with the unknown'.

Rowan Williams has a lot to say about this journey into the darkness, into the absence of God. In fact, he suggests that this experience 'is the only defence religion ever has or ever will have against the charge of cosy fantasy'.[25] He points out that this experience of 'night of the spirit' or the 'dark night of the soul' has often been thought of as a rather exalted kind of religious experience, or a mystical sharing in the sufferings of Christ. But he suggests that the truth is much more devastating. It is the opposite of mysticism, the end of religious experience.

People come to this awareness of darkness or emptiness in different ways. Sometimes it may be the point in our experience of prayer when words, books and techniques are laid aside because they are no longer helpful. I suspect that many of us came to the Society of Friends at this point. Unlike Rowan Williams' diagnosis, we did not necessarily find only 'darkness, and a sense of utter lostness'. For many of us moving into silence came as sense of blessed release from words and images. For others, he suggests, it may be a personal crisis in which the pain and the senselessness of human experience suddenly seems more overwhelmingly true than all the assurances of religious faith and practice. Or it may be when all our work for justice and peace seems pointless in the face of the apparently intractable destructiveness of human beings. And, as we have been suggest-

25 *Open to Judgement*, pp. 98–99.

ing throughout this book, it may be when we find ourselves living at a time of transition, when traditional ways of expressing faith have failed to resonate for us.

I remember quite vividly the experience of visiting Damaris Parker Rhodes when she was dying. I went to say goodbye to her and to thank her for her part in bringing me into the Society of Friends. It was her Swarthmore Lecture, *Truth: a Path not a Possession* that had so impressed me that I felt drawn to explore the possibility that the Quaker Way might be a path for me. In that last meeting with her we talked about our spiritual experiences, our moments of awareness of the numinous. For Damaris a lively sense of the Presence of God has been one of her most precious experiences. Her chief sadness as she approached her death was that she no longer had that vivid awareness. In a broadcast service from Calcutta on 4th November 2007 it was divulged that this sense of the absence of God was also the experience of Mother Teresa in the latter part of her life.

In my more recent experience of illness and increasing disability I think I understand something of that sense of loss. I assume that in any life threatening illness the body uses all available energy to maintain life, and there is little available for the kind of deep sensory awareness of God's Presence that had been so important to Damaris, and also to a lesser extent, to me.

I talked recently with a Friend in our area meeting who had been a tutor responsible for training Macmillan nurses in the care of the dying. I shared with her my experience of wrestling with the theme of this chapter and my reflections on the sense of absence that often seems to be a feature of serious illness and the process of dying. I wondered whether it would be appropriate to write something about this, and to my surprise she urged me to do so. She thought it was important and would be helpful to people who were experiencing a loss of awareness of God's presence during illness, at the very time when it would seem that they most needed to feel it. It may be important to reflect on the fact that two of the Gospel writers record that Jesus himself, dying in great pain and weakness, felt himself bereft of the presence of God.[26]

However it happens, Rowan Williams suggests that the experience is one in which there are no guiding lights in the dark-

[26] Matthew 27:46; Mark 15:34.

ness, no religious experience we can hold on to. We can only do as T.S. Eliot says, drawing on John of the Cross, 'Let the darkness come upon you, which shall be the darkness of God'.[27] As Rowan Williams observes, the sixteenth-century Spanish mystic St John of the Cross analyses the 'dark night' with great clarity. The point at issue, he suggests, is what you are really after. Do you long for mystical or spiritual experience, inner peace, or do you long for God? If we want reality and we genuinely long for God, Rowan Williams suggests, then we must be prepared to have our religious world blown to pieces. 'You must recognise that God is so unlike whatever can be thought or pictured, that when you have got past the stage of self-indulgent religiosity there will be nothing you can securely know or feel. You face a blank: and any attempt to avoid or shy away from it is a return to playing comfortable religious games'.[28]

The experience of being drawn, sometimes very reluctantly, into the way of unknowing, the 'dark night of faith' is an experience that has become a familiar part of the faith journeys of many women today. Feminist theologians and writers who are trying to document what women are saying about their spiritual quest have suggested that they know in their contemporary experience what T.S. Eliot meant when he borrowed the imagery of St John of the Cross, that to 'arrive where you are not' requires a negative way, that 'In order to arrive at what you do not know / You must go by the way of ignorance'.[29]

I suspect that this may well be part of the inward pilgrimage of men as well, but they seem to have written less about it and often seem less able to locate their feelings or express what is happening to them. However, Alan Jones, in his introduction to Soul Making, confesses that he found it increasingly difficult to feel at home with his fellow believers and seriously out of step with many who professed themselves Christians. On the other hand he felt very much at home with many of his 'unbelieving' friends. He writes, 'I feel that as yet, I have nowhere to lay my head'.[30] Where he does feel at home, like Zoë White, is in the ancient form of Christianity expressed in what is known as the 'desert tradition', and in the experience described as the via negativa, the way of unknowing and darkness.

[27] Four Quartets: 'East Coker'. [28] Open to Judgement, p. 96–97. [29] Four Quartets: 'East Coker'. [30] Soul Making, p. 4.

Chris Cook, in the Swarthmore Lecture *Images and Silence*, talked about the immense sadness with which she came to accept the fact that she was no longer 'experiencing the presence of God' in meeting for worship, or indeed anywhere else. As she struggled to understand this new sense of the absence of God she decided that it was part of the way of unknowing, a part of the spiritual journey which Meister Eckhart describes as the journey towards the God who is 'nothing-at-all', the God who cannot be imagined because our knowing has moved beyond images and into the immense silence of God.[31]

It seems clear that for many of us, men as well as women, this letting go of what have become old and outworn images of God, or religious practices that no longer have meaning for us, can be a lonely and painful process. Mary Grey, a Catholic feminist theologian, is one of those who have suggested that for women the desert of unknowing, the 'dark night' of faith is a very real experience. She writes: 'The worst absence of all is the absence of God ... How can there be any way out of the impasse of this Dark Night today?'[32]

Evelyn Underhill, in her painstaking research into the subject of mysticism, suggested that for every experience of inward illumination, of intense awareness of the presence of God, there was a corresponding experience of destitution and negation. 'The states of darkness and illumination coexist over a long period, alternating sharply and rapidly. Many seers and artists pay in this way, by agonising periods of impotence and depression, for each violent outburst of creative energy'.[33] She observed, however, that this alternation between states of illumination and creativity, and darkness and depression, may well be part of our common psychic experience. Any serious study of George Fox's *Journal* reflects this alternation, though traditional Quaker spirituality focuses almost exclusively on illumination and awareness of the presence of God.

Keith Ward, in *A Vision to Pursue*, suggests that most of us in the West are spiritually dispossessed and that the Desert is everywhere. He talks about the crisis in the Christian faith and its traditional formulations. He goes on to argue, as we have done in this book, that science, history and critical thought have changed

---

[31] *Images and Silence*, p. 77–78.
[32] *Redeeming the Dream*, p. 77. [33] *Mysticism*, p. 383

the way we see the world and we cannot ignore them in matters of religious faith. 'But when we manage to come to terms with them without reserve, the religious scene will look very different: strange, largely unknown but vastly exciting'.[34] It may be that Keith Ward is right, that far from being a seldom talked of part of the spiritual journey, the experience of feeling dispossessed or in exile, is actually part of the experience of a great many of us today. In fact, it is what we might expect if we are, as Thomas Berry suggests, 'between two stories'.[35]

Certainly, as I have indicated, many women are aware of going by the way of dispossession. But I am sure that for many men too, this sense that the old and familiar ways of imaging God, of being aware of God, have come to an end, and what the new ways will be is still unknown, so that we are 'in the dark' until the new story becomes a revelation for us, and offers hints and clues as to the way forward. Until then it may be that we have a God who stands back and allows us to do what seeds do in the darkness, to break out of the hard, husk of ourselves, to leave the old protective shell behind, and to grow.

I believe that Annie Dillard gets even nearer to the truth of it when she suggests that it is not so much a case of an absentee God, or even a God who moves off to give us space to be truly ourselves, but a God who has 'spread as our vision and understanding of the universe have spread and become a vast and shimmering web of interconnections, a fabric of spirit, a mysterious and dazzling darkness.'[36]

---

[34] *A Vision to Pursue,* p. 160. [35] *The Dream of the Earth,* p. 123.
[36] *Pilgrim at Tinker Creek,* p. 7.

Chapter 9
Faith in Transition

Alex Wildwood

Faith ... involves a constant search for a deeper awareness of the Divine Mystery, not a holding on to fixed doctrines. In that search today, if we will, we may be illuminated by the insights of all the great spiritual traditions.

Marcus Braybrooke[1]

Faith isn't certainty; it is the courage to live and even celebrate in the midst of uncertainty.

Jonathan Sacks[2]

Belief is the result of mental activity but faith is rooted in the deep biological processes of the body.

Alexander Lowen[3]

The search for ecstasy (meaning 'to go out of or beyond the self') is as old as our humanity; as the only animals with a sense of our own mortality, we need ecstasy and transcendence because the prospect of personal extinction is so hard to bear. This does not mean, as Freud supposed, that religious belief systems are only 'a protection against suffering through a delusional remoulding of reality'.[4] Rather, it means that religion and faith

---

1 *Time to meet*, p. 1. 2 The Chief Rabbi was talking on Radio 4 'Thought for the Day', 20 September 2002. 3 *Depression and the Body*, p. 12; Alexander Lowen was an analyst and bodyworker, founding bioenergetics. 4 *Civilization and its Discontents*, p. 81; also at www.freud. org.uk/education/topic/10573/subtopic/40005/ Quoted by Sharon Salzberg in *Faith*, p. 52.

are natural to human beings, essential in what Karen Armstrong calls 'the struggle for a meaning that will prevent us falling into the crippling despondency to which humanity is prone'. With only six per cent of the population of Britain now attending a religious service of any kind on a regular basis, she observes that 'to profess an allegiance to any faith is becoming increasingly eccentric'. For so many people the God of Western classical theism is indeed dead and can no longer give them what Armstrong identifies as 'the sense of transcendence and ecstasy they need'. At the same time there is currently a huge interest in all things spiritual and 'a great hunger for the sacred'.[5]

As traditional formulations of religious faith increasingly fail to satisfy the spiritual seekers of our postmodern age, and with science itself supplying a source of mystical inspiration as we contemplate the awesome story of our Universe, our understanding of faith itself is also in transition. Whether because we are grieving 'the death of God' or because we are finding awe and wonder outside the structures of traditional religion, the times we live in invite us to embrace what theologian Sara Maitland calls 'a vision of God infinitely bigger, cleverer, wider than our somewhat stunted imaginations have allowed us'.[6]

Part of the current widespread disillusionment with Christianity – especially among the young – is the Church's tendency to equate faith with doctrine and to use faith as a way of determining who belongs 'within the fold'. Dave Tomlinson in his book *The Post-Evangelical* wonders why it is that in an age of almost unparalleled interest in spirituality, the church is still so incredibly unpopular.

Tomlinson identifies several reasons for this unpopularity: one is the mistake of offering today's seekers too neat a package, often a sanitised version of the mystery at the heart of the tradition; another is seeing evangelism as a kind of religious sales operation, depersonalising the listener with a formulaic response. He suggests that evangelism, or 'outreach' to use the Quaker term, is best seen as an opportunity to 'fund people's own spiritual journey', drawing on the 'little pieces of truth' contained in one's own tradition. But the biggest challenge for the Church which he identifies is that the postmodern world is

[5] 'God and the future', in Don Cupitt *et al.*, *Time & Tide*, p. 22–29.
[6] *A Big Enough God?* p. 50

one in which people now reject truth claims which are expressed in the form of dogma or absolutes; one where 'dignity is granted to emotions and intuition, and where people are accustomed to communicating through words linked to images and symbols rather than through plain words or simple statements.' People feel connection with the environment, a strong sense of global unity and suspicion of institutional power. Tomlinson's observations from 1995 seem to be borne out by the rapid emergence of the 'Occupy' movement around the world during 2011 – a global protest which used the technologies of the internet and social media – both crucial aspects of the postmodern sensibility he describes. 'And perhaps most important of all,' he continues, 'it is a world in which the spiritual dimension is once again talked about with great ease'.[7]

In our pluralistic world we need great humility when we talk of faith; Tomlinson names clearly why 'evangelisation' has become a dirty word: 'We all know only in part, we experience only in part, and in a postmodern world it is crucial that we are honest about this limitation'. Because of the contemporary shift away from absolutes, another, broader sense of faith is emerging, one that gets us beyond the argumentation of competing beliefs.

My own struggles to be a person of faith in the early twenty-first century confirm the idea that 'faith is a verb' – the title of a book by Kenneth Stokes, which I came across though Quaker feminist and psychologist Charlotte Davis Kasl, author of books including *Many Roads, One Journey: Moving beyond the twelve steps,* and *Zen and the Art of a Happier Life.* The teacher and writer Sharon Salzberg, coming from the Buddhist tradition, speaks of faith not as something we may possess, but as 'an inner quality that unfolds as we learn to trust our own deepest experience'.[8] She invites us to reclaim faith as something we know experientially. Our faith is something that necessarily grows and changes with age and life experience; the word refers to a developmental process over time within the individual. Yet it also describes the aspirational focus, the shared story and internalised beliefs of a given faith community. So faith is both a quality of living – the journeying itself – and also how we make our own, how we embody the story of human meaning and purpose which we inherit.

[7] *The Post-Evangelical,* pp. 140–41. [8] *Faith: Trusting your own deepest experience,* p. xiv.

Clinical psychologist and former minister David Elkins, in his book *Beyond Religion* refers to the insight of theologian James Fowler – that the Latin word *credo*, usually translated as 'I believe', comes from *cordia* or 'heart' and literally meant 'to set one's heart upon'. Faith is actually best understood as 'an action of the heart rather than an intellectual assent to theological propositions'. To faith (as a verb), Elkins suggests, is to make the effort 'to find a centre for our lives, an ultimate concern that we can believe in and give ourselves to'.[9] Fowler describes faith as 'a way of moving into the force field of our lives', of finding 'an overarching, integrating and grounding trust in a centre of value and power sufficiently worthy to give our lives unity and meaning'.[10]

In that search today our sense of faith – as Quakers – has to be reconciled, at a deep level, with our being products of the Protestant Reformation, with its valorisation of personal conscience, and heirs of the Enlightenment and its scientific rationality. The great swelling tides of secularism have washed over us all; liberation movements born of an impatience for heaven on Earth, for peace and justice here and now and not in some world to come, now inform our religious longings irreversibly. Pluralism, multi-culturalism, the 'information revolution' – all have made us aware as never before of the many religious traditions and human spiritualities of humankind. It is no longer possible to believe ours the only (or unquestioningly the best) path available. This is the reality with which post-doctrinal religion must come to terms.

For me, the Religious Society of Friends is one of the most exciting places to be in this time precisely because in this community we consciously hold the tension between our traditional belief-structure, the Christian roots of our heritage, and the active personal searching and questioning that are the hallmarks of experiential faith. Sharon Salzberg contrasts 'faith' and 'belief' as two approaches to religious life: faith is 'not a definition of reality, not a received answer, but an active, open state that makes us willing to explore. While beliefs come to us from outside – from another person or a tradition or heritage – faith comes from within, from our alive participation in the process of discovery'.[11]

[9] *Beyond Religion*, pp. 29–30. [10] *Stages of Faith*, p. 5.
[11] *Beyond Religion*, p. 67

Our faith then is something deeply personal which we may well have trouble putting into words – yet is the touchstone we can rely upon when adversity takes us by surprise, when something unexpected shatters the gentle equilibrium of our lives. When our daughter Hannah, at age fourteen months was diagnosed with an aggressive and possibly fatal brain tumour, my own ability to trust, to faith, was certainly challenged.

I vividly remember one morning a few days after her initial surgery. We were staying in a cottage in the grounds provided by a charity set up to support parents in our situation. Hannah was in the high dependency unit and my wife and I were taking it in turns to be by her side, day and night. I remember on this bright clear November morning there was a heavy frost on the ground and as I walked towards a huge cedar tree I was struck by the extraordinary vividness, the sense of presence that permeated everything that morning. I was feeling intensely grateful that she had survived this far but was now also painfully aware that there are no guarantees, that all our expectations of what is normal, our sense of what is ours *by right*, bear no relation to what may actually happen in our lives.

I remember being both amazed at the beauty of the scene that morning, the crisp whiteness of the frosted ground beneath my feet, the brilliance of the winter sun in the sky, the majestic ancient presence of this vast evergreen tree as I passed beneath its dipping boughs. And I remember, quite suddenly, even irrationally, an intense anger at all this beauty; I wanted the world to reflect my unhappiness, the devastation we were experiencing as a family. But then, I realised, why should it? What a monstrous conceit on my part. And besides, was I not also, on some other level, deeply heartened that life *does* go on, that although our lives were in turmoil and our hearts had never been heavier, still the sun was shining, still the full force of life on Earth hummed and shimmered and announced itself to me in every encounter, if only I were open to experiencing it?

In that moment I understood something of the necessity of suffering. Not that there is something heroic or intrinsically redemptive about pain and loss: I understood not just the inevitability of suffering but also how at the level of complexity of the human organism, it is the breaking of our hearts through suffering that opens us more fully to Reality, to the truth of our interdependent lives, to the infinitely subtle patterning of things. For it is when we suffer – and don't fall into bitterness – that our hearts are opened, that our isolation is overcome and we transcend our narrow sense of self.

Now when I look back on Hannah's illness and recall the totality of all we experienced – when I do not censor or discount any aspect of it – I hardly know how to characterise it. I cannot call it tragic – primarily because Hannah miraculously survived and continues to thrive – but also because in being present to the whole of it I learnt more deeply than ever before to accept life on its own terms, to be hugely more appreciative of the gift of life, to take nothing for granted and to enjoy each precious present moment I share with those around me. When I include absolutely every part of the experience, remembering the palpable sense of upholding we experienced – the tangible support of prayers and good wishes that sustained us as Friends worldwide (and those from many other faith communities) held us in their hearts and prayers – I recognise the entire episode as a most profound faithing for all of us. Even in the midst of pain and uncertainty, the sense of relationship, of interconnectedness – which in the human realm manifests as loving kindness and compassion – was tangible, felt like a vital expression of life's desire for things to be well.

Through this painful episode I came to realise what Sharon Salzberg meant when she wrote: 'Faith is the animation of the heart that says, "I chose life, I align myself with the potential inherent in life, I give myself over to that potential".'[12] She speaks of 'the power of moving through great heartache and, rather than being destroyed by it, coming to greater faith – faith in one's self, faith in the power of love, faith in the movement of life itself'.[13] This sense of a personal faith-process is far removed from the traditional sense of gaining faith through the acquisition of beliefs, which 'try to make a known out of the unknown', whereas faith 'doesn't carve out reality according to our preconceptions and desires'. It is 'the ability to move forward even without knowing'.[14]

[12] *Beyond Religion*, p. 16. [13] *Ibid.*, p. 109. [14] *Ibid.*, p. 67.

This period in my own life also evoked the double meaning of the title of this chapter: our faithing is how we accept, how we learn to trust, at the deepest level, that the essence of life is transition; that constant movement and change are at the heart of our universe-process. As Daniel Barenboim commented in his Reith lecture in 2006, 'Transition is the basis of human existence',[15] and of course, impermanence is a foundational teaching in Buddhism. Faith and the transience of life are interwoven. This sense of faith-as-process, this discipline of living in the present moment is not to assume everything will turn out all right. Often, of course, things don't 'turn out right'. We may have been blessed that Hannah not only survived but did so with quite minor long-term effects, but three years after her critical illness the child who would have been her younger sister died mysteriously in the womb, was stillborn eight months into the pregnancy. Faith entails our understanding that we simply don't know how things will unfold; but it is faith that 'allows us to claim the possibility that we ourselves might change in ways that will allow us to recognise and trust the helping hands stretched toward us. It enables us to aspire to a better life than the one we have inherited'.[16]

Such faithing challenges us to a radical letting go, a whole-hearted embracing of uncertainty. 'True faith is not assurance, but the readiness to go forward experimentally, without assurance. It is a sensitivity to things not yet known', says Charles Carter in his 1971 Swarthmore lecture.[17] It is our active faithing, Salzberg suggests, that enables us, despite our fear of the unknown, 'to be fully engaged while also realising that we are not in control, and that no strategy can ever put us in control, of the unfolding of events. Faith gives us a willingness to engage life, which means the unknown, and not shrink back from it'.[18]

So it was this kind of faith that was awakened in me on a second cold November morning as we buried our newborn infant in the meeting house grounds. I had dug the grave myself, as something active to do with my grief, some gift to the dead in the labour of the living. But it was only as we lowered the tiny wicker coffin into the ground that I realised there was a further

[15] Daniel Barenboim Reith Lecture Broadcast on BBC Radio 4, May 5th, 2006 [16] *Beyond Religion*, p. 15. [17] *On having a sense of all conditions*, p. 25. [18] *Faith*, p. 87–88

gift in it for me; in that moment I suddenly felt kinship with all those parents around the world whose children were, at that very moment, dying because of war, famine and disease and who have no choice but to dig such simple graves themselves. For the briefest of moments the insulation of my privilege was stripped away and I was brought into grieving intimacy with them all.

Faith as a verb requires that we develop a capacity to observe ourselves, not in a clinical, coldly dispassionate way, but in the sense of having just enough distance not to be overwhelmed, not to be totally absorbed in our own pain and suffering, our momentary experience of reality. Faith is a capacity to open to what is actually happening, to notice the changing texture and tone, the subtle, moment-by-moment evolution of what happens; it is about opening ourselves up to, making room for, even the most difficult experiences.

Both when Hannah was critically ill and when her younger sister died, nothing in what I learnt as religion in my childhood comforted me. I do not believe in an afterlife; I did not imagine our dead child 'held in the arms of Jesus', or 'going to a better place' – as one of our health visitors put it in her well-meaning effort to console us. By surrendering to what was happening, I had the chance to recognise – in a way I might not when things are going well – that we do indeed 'participate in mystery', we are part of something so much vaster than my imagining – and pain and joy, beauty and suffering, are all enfolded in its intricate weave. To accept life is to realise that the price of love is grief, that impermanence is our only certainty, that it is only in the context of a greater, sacred wholeness that we can find meaning in the pain and losses we may each have to bear. The call to faithfulness, I have come to realise, lies precisely in our ability to embrace uncertainty, to live in the confidence that there is an underlying patterning to existence from which nothing, not even death (the ego's terror of oblivion) can ever truly separate us.

I remember being on a workshop with Joanna Macy in 2005 and hearing two things she said that speak of the sense of faith I am exploring here. Central to her work and teaching is the understanding that 'to open to our love of life is to open to the pain of the world'; she quotes the fourteenth century Buddhist sage Shantideva: 'Let all sorrows ripen in me'.

During one of the experiential exercises, a participant was in great distress precisely because she had opened herself to this global dimension of pain, which Joanna ennobles by naming it The Grief, The Suffering of our world (of which our personal suffering is an inseparable part). As this participant lay curled up on the floor sobbing, Joanna gently crouched down beside her and said, with clear authority and conviction, 'There is nothing you can feel, there is nowhere you can go, that can sever you from the living body of the Earth which holds you'. In the sacred intensity of that moment, her words spoke powerfully to many of those present.

On the same workshop at one point there was a discussion in which the question arose, given the cosmic scale of things, given the constant flux and flow of the universe-process, whether it really mattered that human beings are having such a devastating impact on the planet. Joanna simply replied, 'I'm attached to life on Earth; I'm built for that'. Again, it was some time after she spoke that I realised that this was a profound statement of evolutionary faith.

If faith is experienced by many of us today as a radical trust in life itself, then what we are called to is a disciplined presence to the world, to living in awareness of the mystery at the heart of every moment. Being fully present to the ever-changing circumstances of our lives means accepting *everything* our lives present to us; it means taking seriously the advice of theologian and novelist Frederick Buechner:

> Listen to your life. See it for the fathomless mystery it is. In the boredom and the pain of it no less than in the excitement and gladness: touch, taste, smell your way to the holy and hidden heart of it because in the last analysis all moments are key moments, and life itself is grace.[19]

Yet living in our increasingly technological world, the sanitised, virtual reality we have constructed out of a sense of radical separation from the rest of life, it is precisely 'fathomless mystery' from which we have insulated ourselves. The inevitable pain and unpredictability of life, its essential untidiness, its wildness, are seen as things we need to control, as undesirable

---

[19] *Now & Then*, p. 87.

things we try to insure ourselves against. In hospital we sometimes encountered an unspoken belief that death was somehow the enemy, a sign of failure – as if we can collectively pretend that death is negotiable. Yet to embrace the cosmic story of our origins is actually to place ourselves more deeply within the cycles of birth, death and rebirth.

What it would mean to really experience ourselves as 'emerging within and out of the creative dynamics of an evolutionary universe fifteen billion years in the making'? John Surette is a Jesuit, founder of the Spiritearth centre and network, based at The Well, an eco-spirituality centre in Chicago[20]: he reinterprets the Christian story from this perspective. He asks, what if we truly recognised the whole of our selves as progeny of the epic of evolution, not just as physical organisms, but as 'the total feeling, thinking, knowing, creative and worshipping creatures that we are'? The Sun burns up and transforms four million tons of itself every second, which makes most of life on Earth possible. The Sun sacrifices itself each second (death) so that life might come forth on Earth (resurrection). 'Death and resurrection', he concludes, 'are dimensions of the whole Universe', built into the Cosmos, 'how Earth is enlivened, and how our lives unfold. All of the small dyings and risings of our personal lives and our final doing so at our deaths is and will be an activating of this deep dimension within Existence'.[21]

The enterprise of Western civilisation has been, all too often, a denial of our essential embeddedness within the relational matrix of life; religious faith has often been seen as seeking liberation out of the 'constraints' of physical existence. This has kept us in a tragic flight from reality – and had led us to dishonour and desecrate the body of the Earth. Philip Simmons was a contributing editor to the Unitarian Universalist Association who at age 35, with a young family and promising career ahead of him, was diagnosed in 1993 with motor neurone disease, also called Lou Gehrig's disease (a condition that is usually fatal within two to five years), and he died in 2002. In his inspiringly perceptive memoir, *Learning to Fall: the rewards of an imperfect life*, he speaks of the need to 'to choose the world' –

[20] See www.csjthewell.org/ [21] All quotes from his article 'Epic of evolution ... The Jesus connection', *Spiritearth Newsletter*, August 2002, pp. 4–5.

which means embracing all of it: 'the tall maple and the severed stump … In choosing the world we choose both pleasure and pain, joy and sorrow, health and illness, rapture and rue'.[22]

To choose the world means 'to look, and look again, to let ourselves be broken open by its intricacy and mystery'.[23] But being broken open in this way is not really something we can consciously choose. Fortunately life does it for us, whether we feel ready and willing or not. In the words of the twentieth century Jungian analyst, playwright, and suffragist Florida Scott Maxwell:

> Life does not accommodate you, it shatters you. It is meant to, and it couldn't do it better. Every seed destroys its container or else there would be no fruition.[24]

If we are not to 'miss our appointment with life' (in Thich Nhat Hanh's elegant phrase) then it is our experience of faith as being present to the holiness of the ordinary and everyday that we must cultivate. If our aspiration is to simply, whole-heartedly, be present to all that is given us, gratuitously, by the grace of being alive, then we must be willing to 'possess all we have been and done' and to be '*fierce with reality*'.[25] To accept the invitation to be 'fierce with reality', to live in this whole-heartedly faithful way, encouragement may come as much from poets as from theologians or philosophers. In the last stanza of her poem, 'When Death Comes', the Pulitzer prize-winning poet and essayist Mary Oliver captures the urgent poignancy of the call life offers us – not to have been simply a visitor in this world. 'When it's over, I want to say: all my life / I was a bride married to amazement'.[26]

Faith as this kind of radical, accepting presence in and to the world, is ultimately a matter of choice: for the spiritual activist Rabbi Michael Lerner, 'To see the world from the standpoint of the development of Spirit is a faith choice just as seeing it as little more than a jumble of random and indifferent facts is'.[27] In faith I trust that the Mystery in which we participate wishes me, my little human beingness – this one small jewel in the firmament of the visible universe – this Reality wishes me well

22 *Learning to Fall*, p. 93. See www.learningtofall.com   23 *Ibid.*, p. 99.
24 *The measure of my days*, p. 65.   25 *Ibid.*, p. 42.   26 'When Death Comes', *New & Selected Poems*.   27 *Spirit Matters*, pp. 133–34

and supports me as I align myself with its unfolding. Faith, for me, comes down to this: the radical acceptance of my belonging here; it is this recognition of belonging which can give my life meaning and purpose.

Yet I can certainly identify with the sense of loss that many people feel in this post-theistic age, as the old certainties, the familiar language and symbols of religious faith, start to lose their effectiveness. Lacking the familiar kind of faith (faith as 'belief-in') I can easily doubt that I am entitled to speak of faith at all; I can easily feel deficient, as if I lack commitment to the truly religious, surrendered, life. But then I realise what good company I'm in as I am inspired by the new language of an expansive, holistic spirituality. I begin to see beyond my personal sense of emptiness and loss, of failure to be a 'really spiritual' person, or a 'proper Quaker'. I remember that this must be how it feels for many of us 'living between stories', hesitant, waiting, discerning what faithfulness requires of us in this time, even if this looks like 'atheism' – which Karen Armstrong finds has been used during periods of transition, at times when people were making a new leap forward in religious understanding, and it may well be that the prevalent atheism we encounter today will also 'herald the advent of a new form of religious understanding'.[28]

The great religious and wisdom traditions are needed in the coming transformation of human consciousness because it requires both effort and evocation. We are faced with the task of re-visioning ourselves as *planetary beings*; Thomas Berry speaks of this time as a moment of grace – and transient. 'The transformation must take place within a brief period. Otherwise it is gone forever.' In the immense story of the universe, 'so many of these dangerous moments have been navigated successfully is some indication that the universe is for us rather than against us'.[29] To succeed in this task of shaping the future wisely, we need what Berry calls 'the will of the more comprehensive self': 'The individual will can function in this capacity only through an acknowledged union with the deeper structures of reality'.[30]

At our 'Faith in Transition' weekend at Charney Manor in 2006, Jo quoted the twentieth century mystic Simone Weil:

[28] 'God & the Future', in Cupitt *et al.*, *Time & Tide*, p. 26
[29] *The Great Work*, p. 201.   [30] *Ibid.*, p. 173–74

'absolute attention is prayer'.[31] But attention to what? If no longer, for many of us, to a supernatural Other, then attention to something as truly awesome – to the evolving process of the universe itself, manifest in us and within all we see and sense around us. In the listening/sensing spirituality that is called for in this time, our task is to be present to Reality itself as sacred.

[31] See Sallie McFague's commentary on this phrase in her essay 'Consider the Lilies of the Field: How should Christians love nature?'

Chapter 10
Glimpses of a New Spirituality

Jo Farrow

God is neither the puppet master pulling our strings, nor the patriarch in the sky. God is at the centre of our time together, the life pumping through our arteries, the very ground of our being.

Britain Yearly Meeting Epistle, 2005

If we do not recognise the spirituality of all creation; if we do not hear its songs and venerate its beauty, that will be the end of all story and of all song.

Harvey Gillman[1]

I believe this is the opportunity for a new spiritual vision, the seeing of our interconnection with all about us – plants, animals, people.

Anne Bancroft[2]

There are times when I watch a documentary on the Benedictine life, or listen to a programme from Iona, when I long for that lost language of faith, for the scaffolding of religious rites and symbols, for the security of belonging to a way of life buttressed by a thousand years and more of tradition. Being 'a believer in exile', or being what Keith Ward calls one of 'the dispossessed', is not easy. Our new understanding that we live in an

[1] *Consider the Blackbird*, p. 125. [2] *The Spiritual Journey*, p. 126

emergent or continually developing universe is a perception that must transform every religious tradition, he observes in *A Vision to Pursue*, we can no longer assume that a final truth lies in the past, in a special revelation given to some great and prophetic religious leader. This, he suggests, is the perpetual temptation of faith communities, to claim authority for their stance by tracing it back to a mythical beginning located in the past. 'What has to be accepted is the genuineness and importance of the new'.[3]

There is a real bereavement in being, as Zoë White described it, 'deserted by the known'. For John Shelby Spong, 'There is something frightening and lonely about recognising that we can no longer be children dependent on the theistic parent-God'.[4]

There is a sense, however, in which faith is perennially in transition. It was in transition when George Fox and the first generation of Quakers jettisoned traditional ways of worship and more conventional ways of expressing faith. It was in transition when Martin Luther precipitated the Protestant Reformation by publishing his ninety-five Theses. It was in transition when third- and fourth-century religious drop-outs re-invented the monastic way of life. It was in transition when first-century Christians broke away from Judaism and became a new community of faith. We are not, therefore, confronted by a situation that is entirely new and unprecedented. What is new for us is the problem with which Bonhoeffer wrestled in his prison cell, and with which John Robinson wrestled in *Honest to God*, more recently expressed by John Shelby Spong in *A New Christianity for a New World*: namely the problem and opportunity of living in a post-theistic age and what this really means for us as communities of faith.

In his book John Shelby Spong suggests that the time has come when we 'must begin a new exploration into the divine, must sketch out a vision of the holy that is beyond theism but not beyond the reality for which the word God was created to point'.[5] He sees God, not as the external cosmic boss but as the ultimate source of life, the Ground of Being, and suggests that 'One worships this God by living fully, by sharing deeply'.[6] This conclusion was not new by any means.

Less than a year before the Gestapo hanged him, Dietrich Bonhoeffer was writing to a friend about what he called

[3] *A Vision to Pursue*, p. 149. [4] *A New Christianity for a New World*, p. 59. [5] *Ibid.*, p. 55. [6] *Ibid.*, p. 70

'religionless or "worldly" Christianity'. 'Jesus does not call men to a new religion, but to life'.[7] Like many of us he confessed that to begin with he believed that he would discover what faith was all about by trying to live a holy life. Later, and to the end of his life, he came to see that only by living fully and completely in this world would he discover what faith really meant. He had already moved beyond theism, and in his outline of a book he wanted to write he suggested that 'Our relationship to God is not a religious relationship to a supreme Being, absolute in power and goodness, which is a spurious conception of transcendence, but a new life for others, through participation in the Being of God'.[8]

It may feel frightening to leave theistic definitions of God behind, but it may also be a liberating experience. John Shelby Spong once asked a congregation to say what content came to their minds when they heard the word 'God'. He was astonished at their responses. The words that came pouring out were words like 'energy', 'nature', 'love', 'connection', and 'creative strength'.

I sat in our lush, green garden and asked myself the same question. The words that spilled out were 'growth',' change', 'abundance', 'freshness', 'movement', 'beauty', 'vitality', 'miracle', 'light' and 'peace'. I thought of my partner, who works so hard to make this garden such a restful and lovely space, and 'love' and 'companionship' followed hard on my first spontaneous thoughts. I realised that the non-theistic God is all of these things to me, and more. This was my experience when I met with women Friends in New Zealand and we explored spirituality in terms of what was holy for us. The 'holy' was, at that particular moment, a tiny island in Auckland harbour – a sea shore, shells and rocks, trees and greenness, all the rich diversity of the natural world, as well as the experience of being together and communicating our responses and reflections. We were in the process of realising that for us, as a group of women, it was the earth and the natural world, as well as the prime importance of relationships that was the locus of the sacred. It was here that we found our epiphanies and revelations.

[7] *Letters and Papers from Prison*, p. 167. [8] *Ibid.*, p. 179; echoes of this view can be seen in our 2005 Yearly Meeting Epistle.

As I went on writing in our wild, green garden I was equally surprised to find many of the more conventional theological terms coming into my mind – words like 'grace' and 'beatitude', 'glory', 'benediction', and 'sacrament'. They are no longer words that belong in my mind to a supernatural or transcendent frame of reference. They belong to my 'here and now' awareness of being held securely in the Web of Life. I knew, as I wrote, that I was blessed and graced, and I knew, as George Fox knew, that it is the Earth itself, and no sacred building, that is the 'holy place'.[9] The words I once knew in a religious context are no longer part of a theistic scheme of things, interventions of a transcendent God acting from beyond the parameters of my finite life. They are divine processes that belong to the structure of the universe itself. They are part of the ongoing story of evolution and I am a part of that tremendous story. They are the gifts of Life itself, the features of our great cosmic narrative.

In *Sacred Longings* Mary Grey writes about what she calls the 'luminous possibilities of seascape' and suggests that living 'at the edge of the sea's mysteries is one way of experiencing the graced possibilities of sacramental poetics'.[10] In other words she was describing what we had discovered on Waiheki Island, the grace and sacrament of the natural world. She goes on to suggest that 'ecomysticism' is a way of spirituality that is appropriate in a new age in which our planet is under threat as never before. She is one of a host of feminist theologians who have been pleading for a recovery of our sense of connection with the earth and recognition that the universe itself is revelatory.

A spirituality that views all life, human and non-human, and all of creation, as sacred; which treasures and celebrates it and protests against all that diminishes and degrades it, is surely one that is relevant to the problems of the twenty-first century. Nor is it alien to Friends, who from the beginning of their story have held a testimony to the goodness of creation. I have already mentioned the fact that during my first visit to the United States I came across a study scheme on the Quaker Testimonies, published by Friends United Press. The seventh study session was devoted to the 'Testimony to the Goodness of Creation'.[11]

9 *Journal*, (Nickalls ed), pp. 108–09. 10 *Sacred Longings*, p. 96
11 Ben Richmond, *Testimonies*, pp. 22–25

John Yungblut, one time Director of Pendle Hill Quaker Study Centre, wrestled with the need to create a myth to live by. He wrote of the need for 'a spirituality of the earth, an earth mysticism. Not a spirituality directed to the earth, but a spirituality of the earth. I mean this in the sense of evolving naturally from the earth, the earth's own spirituality, and arising out of the earth as we have arisen out of the earth".[12] For Diarmuid O' Murchu, 'Our lives make no sense without an intense connection with the earth itself, and until we reclaim that connection – in a radical way – we'll continue to feel like people in exile, expelled from their true home'.[13]

I understand what he means, and it is underlined for me as I have begun writing this chapter. I am still sitting in our summer house looking out on a garden overflowing with abundance; dozens of shades of green interspersed with the brilliant colours of late summer flowers; and 'grass', which for me has always been a symbol of resurrection. The garden is full of birds – finches and blackbirds, blue tits and great tits, sparrows and starlings, a pair of collared doves and their family, and the occasional wren. And, of course, there is all around me 'earth', teeming with microscopic life in unimaginable thousands of creatures from worms to bacteria.

Bees go about their business of collecting nectar. Small insects scurry to and fro in the grass. And quite suddenly I am aware that I am at peace, content, reconnected with the source of life, at home in a universe of marvels. In fact, as I reflect on it I realise it is more than a sense of deep peace. It is something closer to ecstasy. It needs no words, no scriptures, no sacred building. It is itself the 'holy space', the place of revelation and miracle. The only fitting response for me, since I can no longer dance or sing, is a wondering silence and a huge sense of gratitude. I am no longer an exile. I am at home.

Being reconnected to the source of life is not just about idyllic moments in a wild, green garden. It means knowing at a much deeper level what native Americans mean when they say 'all our relations'. I realised that again when the great bottlenose whale, thousands of miles from home, floundered in the waters of the Thames and seemed unable to find its way back to the

[12] *Shaping a Personal Myth to Live By*, p. 48. [13] *Religion in Exile*, p. 27

open sea. I was surprised to find myself full of an anguished yearning and a sense of affinity with that distressed mammal. The pain I felt for it was like the pain I experienced when my mother was dying. Why was I surprised to feel that connection and that sense of anguish? I have written and spoken often enough about the fact that we live in an interconnected universe and that we are related to everything in it. But those were things I knew in my head, and sometimes in my blood and bones. This sharper sense of connection was 'knowing with my heart' and it was very painful.

I am not denying that there is a very dark side to nature, and if some scientists are right, that dark matter and dark energy constitute at least ninety per cent of the stuff of the universe. But I believe that Mary Grey is right in pleading for what she calls 'ecomysticism', learning to look and listen, living with the paradox of beauty and suffering in the natural world, savagery and extravagant generosity 'as revelatory of the mystery of God everywhere ... of the hallowing of the everyday, of keeping the subsoil in mind'.[14]

Mary Grey goes on to suggest that this kind of spirituality is not individualistic. It is a journey in community. This prompts the question as to how our different faith communities can become spaces where all that we see and hear and learn in this extraordinary universe can be experienced and celebrated. We will need to invent new rituals, or ways of worshipping that will allow space for affirming our solidarity with the suffering earth and with suffering people. She pleads for space in which we can experience a recovery of prophetic lament and grief for all that has disappeared, and yet where we can still give thanks for the vulnerable beauty and wonder that remains, a place where we can commit ourselves to life styles that reflect our concern for the survival and flourishing of threatened peoples.

As Friends we would have no difficulty in accepting the idea of appropriate life styles. But we might have trouble with prophetic lament and celebration. In 1982 Ormerod Greenwood gave the James Backhouse Lecture on the theme of 'Celebration – A Missing Element in Quaker Worship'. In it he recalls the occasion when a Greek folk singer came to Friends House to give a performance designed to raise money for the work of a

14 *Sacred Longings*, p. 168

domestic training school for girls in Salonica, which was, at that time, run by Friends. He remembered that she sang a medley of Greek songs, some melancholy, some gay, and that she performed them not only with her voice but with her body, her eyes, her arms. A Greek audience, he observed, would have responded by clapping to the rhythms, weeping, laughing, dancing, screaming. 'But the stolid rows of Quakers heard her out with unflickering immobility and unshakeable indifference, with no response but polite applause'.[15] That experience of seeing the sharp contrast between the stolid, unemotional response of Friends and the range of emotions expressed in voice and movement by the Greek folk singer made Ormerod Greenwood aware of the fact that though he was a devoted Quaker he was also an unsatisfied one. He became aware that Quakers had somehow become trapped within a limited range of responses that were considered appropriate in worship, and that they had, in fact, set limits to experience.

He was also aware that early Friends were not so constrained, and felt free to express a much wider range of emotional responses. Indeed early Quaker meetings, contrary to popular imaginings, were often very noisy and emotional affairs. But unfortunately Friends ignored the outrage of Fox's widow Margaret Fell, then in her eighties, when she complained bitterly that it was a 'silly poor Gospel', as Friends began to separate themselves from the world, to wear the plain uniform grey that was to characterise them for years, and refused to attend the celebratory feasts and funerals of their non-Quaker neighbours.[16]

Ormerod Greenwood goes on to admit that the practice of holding residential Yearly Meetings had begun to redress the balance, by becoming, unintentionally, celebratory events. He died before we began the experiment of Summer Gatherings, which were much more intentionally celebrations. He would have relished Alex's Swarthmore Lecture in which he pleaded for a 'passionate, juicy Quakerism' and in which he longed for us to become a community of faith 'bringing together science, mysticism and the creative arts in experimental worship, in new forms of celebration and lamentation needed in these exciting and threatening times'.[17]

[15] *Celebration: A Missing Element in Quaker Worship*, p. 3. [16] *Quaker Faith & Practice*, 20.31. [17] *A Faith to Call Our Own*, pp. 98–99.

I am sure that there will be Friends who will say 'where, in all this emphasis on celebration, is the traditional Quaker passion for peacemaking and reconciliation?' In my meeting we have recently completed a series of study groups based on a set of articles on 'Peace' written by David Gee and published by Quaker Peace and Social Witness. In the final article or essay, David Gee writes:

> As a way of 'choosing life', a peace commitment reflects the conviction that the integrity and abundance of life matter. It can begin with the fundamental affirmation of being alive, a celebration of the profusion and integrity of life, and a desire to participate abundantly in it. In this respect, thoughtfulness, creativity and friendship are as integral to peace as political action for social change. Peace is present in the meeting of friends, sharing a meal, reading a book. In this way, a commitment to peace, as shalom (being the wholeness and integrity of life) is more than a moral obligation – an 'ought'. It is a form of creativity in, and with, the whole of life.[18]

In an article in *The Friend* Gordon Smith asks a series of questions that are relevant to the theme of this book. 'Does the new and dramatic understanding of the cosmos not inform Quaker spirituality?' He goes on to ask, 'What better natural sacrament is there than the night sky? ... Does the explosion in the contemporary knowledge of the universe affect us? ... How much attention do we give, as individuals or as a Society, to the heart-stopping images given us by the Hubble space telescope?'[19]

I remember my partner going to a counselling conference on the theme of 'Knowing our story'. Towards the end of the weekend a slide sequence of images from the Hubble space telescope were shown. She said that the impact was mind-blowing. She came home knowing that in some fairly shattering way her life was changed, that she had been made vividly aware that she was part of the awesome story of the Universe itself. Gordon Smith suggests that Friends could invite someone from a local astronomy society to give a slide show, and he goes on to suggest a session at Yearly Meeting. He concludes his article in

18 *Practising Peace*, p. 2. 19 'Stars in your eyes – and in your heart', *The Friend*, 11 July 2003, pp. 10–11.

The Friend: 'Friends, we may live a wonder-filled life. The spirit of worship can indeed be the background of every day. We are all an integral part of this mysterious, incredible cosmos and we can (and do?) know it'.

There are some, such as Richard Holloway,[20] who may feel that a spirituality that reconnects us with the whole of life and allows us no hiding place from its contradictions and uncertainties, its areas of heartache and pain, is a poor exchange for the comforts of a more conventional model. But if we are able to accept the randomness and unknowability of it all, it can give us more than it takes away, as Sara Maitland suggests in *A Big Enough God*:

> We have gained a universe so extraordinary that it should stun us into awe, and a God so magnificently clever and creative that we can have confidence in such a creator's ability to sort out tiny little problems like the resurrection of the body without too much trouble. We are shown a universe that can keep us on our toes, agog with excitement.[21]

The final passage in *Quaker Faith & Practice* challenges us as Friends to accept that we are living at a crucial moment in time when traditional world views no longer satisfy us. But the new thing that is emerging is a coming together of science and mysticism, a rediscovery of the lost creation-centred and mystical tradition within Christianity and a recognition of the spiritual wisdom of native traditions. Grace Blindell asks:

> Are we willing to open ourselves to this wider vision, to cease our urge to control and to listen instead to our hearts, to recognise again the integrity and sacredness of this planet which we have so abused? If we can move from our 'human-sized' viewpoint and look instead from the cosmic viewpoint, there is a sudden and dramatic widening of the lens through which we look. Redemption is seen to be for all creation, and our human story, far from being diminished, is incorporated into the whole drama of an emerging universe.[22]

---

[20] *Looking in the Distance*, p. 107. [21] *A Big Enough God*, p. 62.
[22] *Quaker Faith & Practice*, 29.18

Appendix
The Cosmic Walk

We need to feel this emerging story of the Universe in our hearts as well as with our minds; we need to bring it to life through art, dance and ceremony if it is to become a sacred story for us. When Jo Farrow and I led a weekend at Charney Manor in July 2002 on 'Universe as Revelation', I offered a way of experiencing this story originally devised by Miriam MacGillis.

'The Cosmic Walk' brings home to us the immense journey which is our heritage. It is offered as a walking meditation, something experienced in our bodies and through our senses, a way of taking us beyond conceptual understanding into deep levels of inner knowing. It is a form of evolutionary re-membering which helps change our perception of who we are. Mary Coelho, one of those who has been developing this practice, writes:

> We need great acts of imagination, of intuitive perception and celebration to help us embrace the revelatory material being offered us. The Cosmic Walk … is a symbolic re-enactment that helps us enter personally into the story.[1]

Silently, a group of people walk together, the silence punctuated by the occasional commentary of a Narrator who invites us to mark the significant milestones of our journey through space and time. One version of the Prologue which I find particularly inspiring begins:

> Thirteen billion years ago, from that place that was no-place, from that time that was no-time, the cosmos flared forth in a silent blaze of inconceivable brilliance. All the energy that would ever exist in the entire course of time erupted from a point smaller than a grain of sand. Unimaginable vast quantities of elementary particles, lights, and space-time itself, unfurled and expanded from this quantum vacuum, this

[1] From the introduction to a version of the Cosmic Walk adapted by Ruth Rosenhek at http://www.rainforestinfo.org.au/deep-eco/cosmic.htm

unity of origination. If in the future, stars would blaze and lizards would blink in their lights, these actions would be powered by the same luminous energy that burst forth at the dawn of time.[2]

When this practice is walked indoors, the path can be followed as a spiral laid out on the floor, with 'stations' along the way marked by candles. When walked outside, participants are reminded by birdsong and the evidence of the season that this is a story we share with all the creatures and elements of our world. In its full form outdoors, the Walk follows a route of 1.4 kilometres, where each metre represents ten million years of our evolutionary journey. This means that each step we take is five million years passing. In all it takes 2,940 steps to complete this ancestral pilgrimage.[3]

Along the way we note the great transitions: after a long time walking in silence, moving through the first two billion years of our story, we honour the emergence of the first atomic building blocks of the universe, the birthing of hydrogen and helium. After another seven billion years (fourteen hundred footfalls) we bear witness to the emergence of the hundred billion galaxies, including our own. Walking on in silent reflection, staying present to the immensity of this journey, we reach the point where roughly five billion years ago our sun's mother star exploded in a supernova dispersing new elemental powers in all directions. The universe adventure deepens with the birth of our sun and, a hundred million years later, the formation of the Earth.

As we proceed, experiencing the unfolding of this Great Story, we note the significant 'anniversaries' along the way. First, the coming of the rains, the exchange between atmosphere and ocean that provided the creative chemical womb that eventually, roughly four billion years ago, brought forth the first living cells, a new step in the development of our universe. We honour the coming of photosynthesis and the crisis that the spread of poisonous quantities of oxygen presented. We witness the emer-

[2] Claudia McNeil & Paulita Bernay, *The Cosmic Walk*; and see www.threeeyesofuniverse.org (search for 'threeeyesofuniverse' and 'cosmic walk'). [3] For a detailed account of background and practicalities of this form, see *Walking the Sacred Story: a new ritual for celebrating the Universe* by Erna & Michael Colebrook, GreenSpirit Pamphlet No. 5, Association for Creation Spirituality, 2000

gence, two billion years ago, of the first distinct living beings, complex cells with nuclei and the capacity to harness oxygen and use it for their own evolutionary purposes. What is striking as we walk is just how long we spent as simple cells, how resilient and dominant a life-form bacteria have proved to be.

We are reminded by the Narrator how six hundred million years ago single-celled creatures merged themselves into the first multi-cellular beings. We silently bear witness to that astonishing moment when the first eyes evolved; we celebrate the first time life on Earth saw itself. The story of life's developing abundance now picks up pace. We witness the development of backbones to protect the earliest nervous systems. We hear of how insects, cooling themselves by fanning heat away from their bodies, unexpectedly took off and became the first creatures to inhabit the sky.

From tracing the formation of limbs first devised to swim, we now remember how fish followed plants and insects onto the land, and soon the continents are heaving with amphibians and reptiles. In a relatively short while, we are walking through the age of the dinosaurs. And as we approach our own more immediate forbears, the scale of our walking meditation changes; we move from a scale of tens of millions to hundreds of thousands of years – and finally to centuries. After such a graphic enactment of life's evolving diversity, the very last footfall has to be slowed down and imagined bit by bit.

Ten centimetres into this last step and we can salute *Australopithecus*, a smallish ape walking on two legs, who emerges in Africa four million years ago. Ten centimetres more and Homo habilis emerges, also in Africa and starts making and using tools. Just 25 millimetres from the end of our journey *Homo sapiens* – our own species – appears. The last thousandth of this last step – the last half a millimetre of our Walk of nearly one and a half kilometres – represents the total span of human history.

The Cosmic Walk is a truly humbling experience but one that also energises us as we sense our full inheritance. *Sensing ourselves* within the one great story of the universe gives us a sense of our true identity. It empowers us to engage in what Thomas Berry calls 'The Great Work' of our age, that of creating 'a mutually sustaining relationship' between humans and the life-community of Earth.

Bibliography

Abram, David, *The Spell of the Sensuous: Perception and language in a more-than-human world.* New York: Vintage, 2007.

Abram, David, *Becoming Animal: An earthly cosmology.* Vintage Books, 2011.

Advices & Queries: published in *Quaker Faith & Practice* as section 1.02 and also as a separate pamphlet. Britain Yearly Meeting of the Religious Society of Friends, 1995 and subsequent editions.

Armstrong, Karen, 'God and the future', in Don Cupitt *et al.*, *Time & Tide: Sea of Faith beyond the millennium.* O Books, 2001.

Ashworth, Timothy, and Alex Wildwood, *Rooted in Christianity, Open to New Light: Quaker spiritual diversity.* Pronoun Press/Woodbrooke, 2009.

Bancroft, Anne, *The Spiritual Journey.* Element, 1991.

Barenboim, Daniel, Reith lecture Broadcast on BBC Radio 4, May 5th, 2006: www.bbc.co.uk/radio4/features/the-reith-lectures/transcripts

Barlow, Connie: www.thegreatstory.org

Bateson, Gregory *Steps to an ecology of mind.* University Of Chicago Press, 1972. Text also at http://mediaecologies.wordpress.com/2008/05/21/bateson-steps-to-an-ecology-of-mind/

Berry, Thomas: www.thomasberry.org

Berry, Thomas, *The Dream of the Earth*, Sierra Club Books, 1988.

Berry, Thomas, and Brian Swimme, *The Universe Story: a celebration of the unfolding of the Cosmos.* HarperSanFrancisco, 1992.

Berry, Thomas, *The Great Work: our way into the future.* Bell Tower/Random House, 1999.

Berry, Thomas, *The Great Story,* video, (Nancy Stetson & Penny Morrell), Bullfrog Films, 2002.

Berry, Thomas, Foreword to: Thomas Merton, *When the Trees Say Nothing: Writings on nature,* ed. Kathleen Deignan. Notre Dame, IN: Sorin Books, 2003.

Birchard, Bruce, *The Burning One-ness Binding Everything* (Pendle Hill Pamphlet 332). Wallingford, PA: Pendle Hill, 1997.

Birkel, Michael L., *Engaging Scripture: reading the Bible with Early Friends*. Richmond, IN: Friends United Press, 2005.

Bloom, Anthony (Metropolitan Anthony of Sourozh), *The Essence of Prayer*. Darton, Longman & Todd, 1986.

Bloom, William, *Soulution: The holistic manifesto*. Hay House, 2004.

Bloom, William: www.f4hs.org/ (website for holistic spirituality).

Bonhoeffer, Dietrich, *Letters and Papers from Prison*. SCM Press, 1953.

Borg, Marcus J., *Reading the Bible Again for the First Time: Taking the Bible seriously but not literally*. HarperSanFrancisco, 2001.

Braybrooke, Marcus, *Time to meet: towards a deeper relationship between Jews and Christians*. London, SCM, 1990.

Brindle, Susannah Kay, 'Quakers & the Australian Community of Nature' in *As the Seed Grows: Essays in Quaker thought*. Australia Yearly Meeting [Religious Society of Friends], 1997.

Brindle, Susannah Kay, *To Learn a New Song*. Australia Yearly Meeting, Backhouse lecture, 2000.

Brindle, Susannah Kay, 'Earth and Quakers', Part 1, *The Australian Friend*, March 2005.

Brindle, Susannah Kay, 'Earth and Quakers', Part 2, *The Australian Friend*, September 2005.

Britain Yearly Meeting of the Religious Society of Friends, *Quaker Faith & Practice*. Britain Yearly Meeting, 1995; revised to 4th ed., 2009.

Britain Yearly Meeting of the Religious Society of Friends, Minute 36 of the Yearly Meeting, 2001, Canterbury; produced as a separate leaflet *Our Canterbury Commitment*, in October 2011 and available from publications@quaker.org.uk and at www.quaker.org.uk/sites/default/files/Minute-36-YMG-2011.pdf

Britain Yearly Meeting of the Religious Society of Friends, Epistle from Yearly Meeting, 2005, York.

Brown, Callum, *The Death of Christian Britain: Understanding secularisation 1800-2000*. London, Routledge, 2001.

Brown, Lester, *Plan B 3.0*. W.W.Norton, 2008.

Bibliography

Buechner, Frederick, *Now & Then.* Harper & Row, 1983; repr. Harper SanFrancisco, 1991

Burnell, Jocelyn, interview with Alison Leonard in *Living in Godless Times.* Floris Books, 2001.

Byrne, Lavinia, *Women Before God.* SPCK, 1988.

Cadman, David, 'Enfolded in every moment', *The Friends' Quarterly*, 2001 issue 3.

Capra, Frijtof, *The Tao of Physics.* Shambhala, 1975.

Capra, Fritjof and David Steindl-Rast, *Belonging to the Universe.* HarperSanFrancisco, 1991.

Carrette, Jeremy, and Richard King, *Selling Spirituality: The silent takeover of religion.* Routledge, 2005.

Carson, Rachel, *Silent Spring.* First published in 1962; Penguin Classics edition, 2000.

Carter, Charles, *On Having a Sense of All Conditions* (Swarthmore Lecture). Friends Home Service Committee, 1971.

Chopra, Deepak, *How to Know God.* Rider 2000.

Christ, Carol P. and Judith Plaskow, eds, *Womanspirit Rising: A feminist reader.* Harper & Row, 1979.

Christ, Carol P., *Rebirth of the Goddess: Finding meaning in feminist spirituality.* Routledge, 1997.

Clarke, Chris, ed., *Ways of Knowing: Science and mysticism today.* Exeter: Imprint Academic, 2005.

Colebrook, Erna, and Michael Colebrook, *Walking the Sacred Story: A new ritual for celebrating the universe*, GreenSpirit Pamphlet No.5, 2000, downloadable from http://www.greenspirit.org.uk/resources/e-books.shtml

Cook, Chris, and Brenda Clifft Heales, *Images and Silence* (Swarthmore Lecture). QHS, 1992.

Cullinan, Cormac, *Wild Law.* Siber Ink, 2002.

Cupitt, Don, *Solar Ethics.* SCM Press, 1995.

Cupitt, Don *et al.*, eds, *Time & Tide: Sea of Faith beyond the millennium.* O Books 2001.

Dale, Jonathan, *Beyond the Spirit of the Age* (Swarthmore Lecture). QHS, 1996.

Davies, Paul, *The Mind of God.* Simon & Schuster, 1992.

Bibliography

Davies, Paul, *The Goldilocks Enigma: Why is the Universe just right for life?* Allen Lane, 2006.

Davison, Steven, '9½ Principles of Christian Earth Stewardship' in *Becoming a Friend to the Creation: Earthcare Leaven for Friends and Friends' Meetings.* Friends Committee on Unity with Nature, 1994.

Dawes, Joycelin, Janice Dolley and Ike Isaksen, *The Quest: Exploring a sense of soul.* O Books, 2005.

d'Espagnat, Bernard, 'Quantum weirdness: what we call reality is just a state of mind', http://www.guardian.co.uk/science/blog/2009/mar/17/templeton-quantum-entanglement

Dillard, Annie, *Pilgrim at Tinker Creek.* Picador, 1976; Canterbury Press, 2001.

Dowd, Michael, *EarthSpirit: A handbook for nurturing an ecological Christianity.* Twenty-third Publications, 1991.

Dowd, Michael, Seattle address, 2002.

Dowd, Michael, *Thank God for Evolution: How the marriage of science and religion will transform your life and our world.* Viking, 2007.

Dowd, Michael: www.thankgodforevolution.com/category/blog

Dyson, Freeman, *Infinite in All Directions.* Harper & Row, 1988.

Easlea, Brian, *Science and Sexual Oppression: Patriarchy's Confrontation with Woman and Nature.* Weidenfeld & Nicholson, 1981.

Ecopsychology: Restoring the Earth, healing the mind, (eds) Theodore Roszak, Mary Gomes & Allen D. Kanner, Sierra Club Books, 1995.

Elgin, Duane, *Promise Ahead: A vision of hope and action for humanity's future.* Quill/HarperCollins, 2000.

Elgin, Duane, *An Incomplete Guide to the Future.* Stanford, 1976.

Eliot, T.S., 'Four Quartets', in *Collected Poems 1909–1962.* Faber, 1963.

Elkins, David, *Beyond Religion: A personal program for building a spiritual life outside the walls of traditional religion.* Wheaton, Illinois: Quest Books, 1998.

Estes, Clarissa Pinkola, *Women who Run with the Wolves.* Rider, 1992.

The Extinction Website: www.petemaas/nl/extinct/

Farrow, Jo, *The World in My Heart: A personal exploration of spirituality and awareness.* Quaker Home Service, 1990.

Bibliography

Fell, Margaret (Margaret Fox), in *Quaker Faith and Practice*, 20.31, Yearly Meeting of the Religious Society of Friends, (Quakers), 1995.

Ferguson, Duncan S., (ed.). *New Age Spirituality: An assessment.* Westminster/John Knox Press, 1993.

Fitch, Joan, *The Present Tense: A discussion paper for Quakers.* Birmingham: Woodbrooke College, 1980.

Ford, Adam, *Universe: God, Man and Science.* Hodder & Stoughton, 1986.

Forman, Robert, *Grassroots Spirituality: What it is, why it is here, where it is going.* Exeter: Imprint Academic, 2004.

Fowler, J., *Stages of Faith.* HarperSanFrancisco, 1981.

Fox, George, *The Journal of George Fox,* revised edition, John L. Nickalls. Cambridge University Press for Religious Society of Friends (London Yearly Meeting), 1952, and later reprints.

Fox, George, *No More but My Love: Letters of George Fox, Quaker,* (ed) Cecil W Sharman. Quaker Home Service, 1980.

Fox, Matthew, website: matthewfox.org

Fox, Matthew, *Original Blessing.* Bear & Co, 1983.

Fox, Matthew, *The Coming of the Cosmic Christ,* Harper & Row, 1988.

Fox, Matthew, *A Spirituality Named Compassion.* Harper & Row, 1990.

Fox, Matthew, *Creation Spirituality: liberating gifts for the peoples of the Earth.* HarperSanFrancisco, 1991.

Fox, Matthew, *Easter Mysteries.* Findhorn Foundation Conference Series, 1991.

Fox, Matthew, 'Spirituality for a new era' in *New Age Spirituality: An assessment,* ed. Duncan S. Ferguson. Westminster/John Knox Press 1993.

Fox, Matthew, *Confessions: the making of a post-denominational priest.* HarperSanFrancisco, 1996.

Fox, Matthew & Sheldrake, Rupert, *Natural Grace,* Bloomsbury, 1997.

Fox, Matthew, *Sins of the Spirit, Blessings of the Flesh.* Gateway, 2000.

Freud, Sigmund, *Civilization and its Discontents,* New York: W.W. Norton, 1961.

Gee, David, *Practising Peace.* Quaker Peace & Social Witness, 2005.

Bibliography

Genesis Farm, www.genesisfarm.org

Gillman, Harvey, *Consider the Blackbird: Reflections on spirituality and language,* Quaker Books, 2007.

Goldenberg, Naomi R., *Changing of the Gods: Feminism and the end of traditional religions.* Beacon Press, 1979.

Gore, Al, *Earth in the Balance: Forging a new common purpose,* originally published 1992, revised ed. Earthscan, 2007.

Gottlieb, Roger, 'Spiritual Deep Ecology and World Religions: a Shared Fate, a Shared Task', in *Deep Ecology and World Religions: New Essays on Sacred Ground.* State Univ. of New York Press, 2001.

Gottlieb, Roger S., ed. *This Sacred Earth: Religion, nature, environment.* London: Routledge, 1996.

The Great Story, website: www.thegreatstory.com

Great Turning Times, www.greatturningtimes.org

Greenwood, J. Ormerod, *Celebration: A missing element in Quaker worship* (18th James Backhouse Lecture). Religious Society of Friends (Quakers) in Australia, 1982.

Grey, Mary, *Redeeming the Dream.* SPCK, 1989.

Grey, Mary, *Sacred Longings.* SCM Press, 2003.

Gribbin, John, *Space.* BBC Books, 2001.

Griffiths, Bede, *A New Vision of Reality.* Collins, 1989.

Grims, John, 'Time, History, Historians in Thomas Berry's Vision', www.thomasberry.org/biography

Harding, Stephan, *Animate Earth: Science, intuition and Gaia.* Green Books, 2009.

Harman, Willis W., *An Incomplete guide to the future.* Stanford, 1976.

Hartmann, Thom, *The Last hours of Ancient Sunlight: Waking up to personal and global transformation.* Hodder & Stoughton, 2001.

Havel, Vaclav, *Disturbing the Peace.* Vintage, 1991.

Hawken, Paul, *Blessed Unrest: How the largest social movement in the world is restoring grace, justice and beauty to the world.* Penguin Books, 2008.

Hay, David, & Hunt, Kate, 'Is Britain's soul waking up?' *The Tablet,* 24 June 2000, p. 846.

Heathfield, Margaret, *Being Together* (Swarthmore Lecture). QHS, 1994.

Heelas, Paul, & Woodhead, Linda, *The Spiritual Revolution: why religion is giving way to spirituality*, Blackwell Publishing, 2005.

Helmuth, Keith, 'The Market Economy as a Spiritual Concern' in *Becoming a Friend to the Creation: Earthcare leaven for Friends and Friends' meetings'*. Friends Committee on Unity with Nature, 1994.

Heron, Alastair, *Our Quaker Tradition*. Curlew Productions, 1999.

Holdsworth, Christopher, *Steps in a Large Room* (Swarthmore Lecture). QHS, 1985.

Holloway, Richard, *Looking in the Distance*. Canongate, 2004.

Ingle, Larry, *First among Friends: George Fox and the creation of Quakerism*. Oxford University Press, 1994.

Jamison, Christopher (Abbot), *Finding Sanctuary: Monastic steps for everyday life*. Weidenfeld & Nicolson, 2006.

Jensen, Derrick, *A Language Older Than Words*. London: Souvenir Press 2002

Johnson, Elizabeth A., *Women, Earth & Creator Spirit* (The Madeleva lecture). Paulist Press, 1993.

Johnson, Elizabeth A., *EarthLight* magazine, vol 25, Spring 1997.

Johnstone, Chris, *Find Your Power*. Nicholas Brealey, 2006; 2nd edition Permanent Publications, 2010. Chris Johnstone was formerly editor of *The Great Turning Times* email newsletter, www.greatturningtimes.org

Jones, Alan, *Soul Making*. SCM Press, 1985.

Kasl, Charlotte Davis, *Many Roads, One Journey : Moving beyond the twelve steps*. New York: HarperPerennial, 1992.

Kasl, Charlotte Davis, *Zen and the Art of a Happier Life*. Random House, 2005.

Keenan, Brian, *An Evil Cradling*. Hutchinson, 1992.

Kelly, Thomas: section 2.40 in *Quaker Faith and Practice,* 1995; from *The Gathered Meeting*, 1940; repr. in *The Eternal Promise*, 1996.

Ketterer, Rose: section 26.35 in *Quaker Faith and Practice,* 1995; from 'G-d/ess Web' in *Friendly Woman* vol.8 (1987) no.1.

Kindred Spirit magazine: www.kindredspirit.co.uk

King, Ursula, *The Search for Spirituality: Our global quest for a spiritual life*. Canterbury Press, 2009.

Koestler, Arthur, *The Ghost in the Machine*. Hutchinson, 1967.

Bibliography

Kowalski, Gary, *Science and the Search for God*. Lantern Books, 2003.

Lampen, John, *Wait in the Light: The Spirituality of George Fox*. QHS, 1981.

Laszlo, Ervin, *Science and the Re-enchantment of the Cosmos: The rise of the integral vision of reality*. Inner Traditions, 2006.

Leibniz, Gottfried Wilhelm, *Philosophical Papers and Letters*, ed. Leroy E. Loemker. Chicago University Press, 1956.

Leonard, Alison, *Living in Godless Times*. Floris Books, 2001.

Leopold, Aldo, *A Sand County Almanac*. Oxford University Press, 1968.

Lerner, Michael, *Spirit Matters*. Charlottesville, VA: Hampton Roads Publishing Co., 2000.

Lewis, C.S., *The Poems of C.S. Lewis*. Geoffrey Bles, 1964.

Loring, Patricia, *Listening Spirituality: Personal* (Vol 1) and *Corporate* (Vol 2) *Spiritual Practices Among Friends*. Washington, Openings Press, 1997 and 1999.

Lovelock, James, *The Ages of Gaia: A biography of our living Earth*. Oxford University Press, 1989.

Lovelock, James, *The Revenge of Gaia: Why the Earth is fighting back – and how we can still save humanity*. Allen Lane/Penguin, 2006.

Lovelock, James, *The Vanishing Face of Gaia: A final warning*. Allen Lane/Penguin, 2010.

Lowen, Alexander, *Depression and the Body*. Penguin, 1973; repr. Bioenergetics Press.

Lunn, Pam, *Costing not less than everything: sustainability and spirituality in challenging times*, Quaker Books, 2011.

MacMurray, John, *The Search for Reality in Religion* (Swarthmore Lecture), QHS, 1965; reprinted 1995.

Macy, Joanna, www.joannamacy.net

Macy, Joanna, *Despair and Personal Power in the Nuclear Age*. New Society Publishers, 1983.

Macy, Joanna, jt author with John Seed *et al.* of *Thinking Like a Mountain: Towards a council of all beings*. New Society Publishers, 1988.

Macy, Joanna, *World as Lover, World as Self*. Berkeley CA: Parallax Press, 1991.

Macy, Joanna, & Young Brown, Molly, *Coming Back to Life: Practices to reconnect our lives, our world*. New Society Publishers, 1998.

Mahon, Tom, *A History of the Universe by Edward, the oldest electron there ever was*, Amazon ebooks.

Maitland, Sara, *A Big Enough God?* Mowbray, 1995.

Mander, Jerry, *In the Absence of the Sacred*. San Francisco: Sierra Club Books, 1991.

Margolin, Malcolm, *The Ohlone Way*, Heyday Books, 1978.

Margulis, Lynn, 'Gaia is tough bitch', www.edge.org/documents/ ThirdCulture/n-Ch.7.html

Massey, Marshall, *Seeking the Kingdom* (Sunderland P. Gardner lecture). Canadian Yearly Meeting [Religious Society of Friends], 1989.

Massey, Marshall, *The Defense of The Peaceable Kingdom* (Social Order Series). Pacific Yearly Meeting [Religious Society of Friends], 1985.

Massey, Marshall, *Seeking the Kingdom*. 1989.

Massey, Marshall, 'Uniting Friends with Nature'. *Friends Bulletin*, October 1985.

Maxwell, Florida Scott, *The measure of my days*, Knopf, 1968.

MacGillis, Miriam, www.genesisfarm.org

MacGillis, Miriam, 'The New Cosmology: its implications for our lives'. Talk given at St James's Church, Piccadilly, London, March 17th 1998; tape, formerly available through www. greenspirit.org.uk/books/ Email greenspiritbooks@btinternet. com for similar material.

MacGillis, Miriam, www.threeeyesofuniverse.org/public/ cosmicwalks/StillPointRetreatCenterSeat.pdf gives details of versions of the ritual form devised by Miriam McGillis.

McFague, Sallie, *Models of God*. SCM Press, 1987.

McFague, Sallie, 'Consider the Lilies of the Field: How should Christians love nature?' in Schwartzenruber, Michael, ed., *The Emerging Christian Way*. Northstone Publishing, 2006.

McLaughlin, Nellie, *Out of Wonder: The evolving story of the universe*. Veritas Publications, 2004.

Merchant, Carolyn, *The Death of Nature: Women, ecology and the scientific revolution*. San Francisco: HarperCollins, 1980.

Merchant, Carolyn, 'The Scientific Revolution and The Death of Nature' http://nature.berkeley.edu/departments/espm/env- hist/articles/84.pdf

Bibliography

Merton, Thomas, *When the Trees Say Nothing: Writings on nature*, ed. Kathleen Deignan, with Foreword by Thomas Berry. Notre Dame, IN: Sorin Books, 2003.

Miles, Margaret R., *The Image and Practice of Holiness*. SCM Press, 1988.

Moltmann, Jurgen, *Spirit of Life*. SCM Press, 1992.

Moore, Thomas, *Care of the Soul*. Piatkus, 1992.

Moore, Thomas, *The Soul's Religion*. Bantam, 2003.

Moore, Thomas, *Dark Nights of the Soul: A Guide to Finding Your Way Through Life's Ordeals,* Piatkus, 2004.

Moore, Thomas, *Care of the Soul in Medicine: Healing Guidance for Patients, Families, and the People Who Care for Them*. Hay House, 2011.

Murgatroyd, Linda, 'The Future of Quakers in Britain'. *The Friends Quarterly*, 2010 issue 2.

Newbigin, Lesslie, *The Household of God: Lectures on the nature of Church*. SCM Press, 1953.

Nolan, Albert, *Jesus Today: A spirituality of radical freedom*. Orbis Books, 2009.

Ochs, Carol, *Women and Spirituality*. Rowman & Littlefield, 1983.

Occupy: http://occupywallst.org/

O'Donohue, John, 'The Priestliness of the Human Heart'. *The Way* [a journal of contemporary spirituality published by the British Jesuits], Supplement 83, 1995. www.theway.org.uk/Back/s083ODonohue.pdf

Oliver, Mary, *New & Selected Poems*. Boston: Beacon Press, 1992.

O' Murchu, Diarmuid, *Religion in Exile*. Crossroad Publishing Company, 2000.

O' Murchu, Diarmuid, *Quantum Theology*. Crossroads Publishing Company, 2004.

Parker Rhodes, Damaris, *Truth: a Path not a Possession* (Swarthmore Lecture). Friends Home Service Committee, 1977. Much of this was later incorporated into her later book *The Way Out is the Way In*. QHS, 1985.

Peck, M. Scott, *The Road Less Travelled*. Simon & Schuster, 1978.

Permaculture Magazine : inspiration for sustainable living, www.permaculture.co.uk

Phipps, Carter, 'A theologian of renewal'. *EnlightenmentNext* magazine, Dec 2008–Feb 2009.

Pink Dandelion, Ben, *A Sociological Analysis of the Theology of Quakers*. Edwin Mellon Press, 1996.

Positive News, www.positivenews.org.uk

Primack, Joel, and Nancy Ellen Abrams, *The View from the Centre of the universe: discovering our extraordinary place in the Cosmos*. Fourth Estate, 2006.

Primavesi, Anne, *Making God laugh*. Polebridge Press, 2004.

Punshon, John, *Testimony and Tradition* (Swarthmore Lecture). QHS, 1990.

Radical Academy, biography of Francis Bacon at radicalacademy. com/philfrancisbacon.htm.

Raine, Kathleen, *Collected Poems*. Hamish Hamilton, 1963.

Reagan, Michael, ed., *The Hand of God: thoughts and images reflecting the Spirit of the Universe*. Templeton Foundation Press/ Lionheart Books, 1999.

Reagan, Michael, ed., *Reflections on the nature of God*. Templeton Foundation Press/Lionheart Books, 2004.

Red List www.iucn/redlist.org

Rees, Martin, *Just Six Numbers: The dark forces that shape the universe*. Phoenix, 2000.

Resurgence magazine: www.resurgence.org

Richmond, Ben, *Testimonies*; edited with teacher notes by Patricia Edwards-Delancey. Friends United Press, 1987.

Rising Tide, *Beyond Oil: The oil curse and solutions for an oil-free future*. Pamphlet by Rising Tide is an Oxford-based action group on climate change; available on www.planB.org

Robinson, John, *Honest to God*. SCM Press, 1963.

Roszak, Theodore, Gomes, Mary, and Kanner, Allen D. (eds), *Ecopsychology: restoring the Earth, healing the mind*. Sierra Club Books, 1995.

Ruether, Rosemary Radford, *Sexism and God-Talk*. SCM Press, 1983.

Runcorn, David, *Rumours of Life*. Darton, Longman & Todd, 1986.

Russell, Peter, *From Science to God: A physicist's journey into the mystery of consciousness*, New World Library, 2002.

Sacks, Jonathan, 'Rabbi Jonathan Sachs on Fundamentalism'. Posted on YouTube by JINSIDER.

Sacred Hoop magazine: www.sacredhoop.org/

Salzberg, Sharon, *Faith: Trusting your own deepest experience.* Element/HarperCollins, 2002.

Schwartzenruber, Michael, ed. *The Emerging Christian Way*, Northstone Publishing, 2006. Contains essay by Sallie McFague, 'Consider the Lilies of the Field: How should Christians love nature?'

Scott, Janet, *What Canst Thou say?* (Swarthmore Lecture). QHS, 1980.

Seed, John, *et al. Thinking Like a Mountain: Towards a council of all beings.* New Society Publishers, 1988.

Senge, Peter, *The Necessary Revolution: How individuals and organizations are working together to create a sustainable world,* Nicholas Brealey, 2010.

Shepard, Paul, 'Ecology and Man', in Shepard and McKinley, eds., *The Subversive Science: Essays toward an ecology of man*, Boston: Houghton Mifflin, 1969.

Shepard, Paul, *Nature and Madness.* San Francisco: Sierra Club, 1982.

Shiva, Vandana, *Water Wars: Privatization, pollution, and profit.* South End Press, 2002

Simmons, Philip, *Learning to Fall: The rewards of an imperfect life.* Hodder Mobius, 2002:93. See www.learningtofall.com

The Sixth Extinction: www.petermaas/nl/extinct/

Slee, Nicola, *Faith & Feminism: an introduction to Christian Feminist theology,* Darton, Longman & Todd, 2003.

Smith, Gordon, 'Stars in your eyes – and in your heart', *The Friend,* 11 July 2003, pp. 10–11.

Spears, Joanne and Larry, *Friendly Bible Study.* Friends General Conference, 1990.

Spong, John Shelby, *Why Christianity Must Change or Die: A bishop speaks to believers in exile.* HarperSanFrancisco, 1998.

Spong, John Shelby, *A New Christianity for a New World.* Harper Collins, 2001.

Spretnak, Charlene, *The Spiritual Dimension of Green Politics.* Bear & Co, 1987.

Starhawk, *The Spiral Dance: A rebirth of the ancient religion of the Great Goddess.* Harper & Row, 1979.

Starhawk, *The Earth Path.* Harper San Francisco, 2004.

Steere, Douglas, *On Listening to Another.* New York: Harper & Brothers, 1955.

Steere, Douglas (ed.), *Quaker Spirituality: Selected Writings* (Classics of Western Spirituality Series). Paulist Press and SPCK, 1984; repr. HarperCollins, 2005.

Stetson, Nancy, and Penny Morrell (producers), *The Great Story* (video). Bullfrog Films 2002.

Steven, Helen, *No Extraordinary Power* (Swarthmore Lecture). Quaker Books, 2005.

Stokes, Kenneth, *Faith is A Verb: Dynamics of Adult Faith Development.* Mystic, CT.: Twenty-Third Publications, 1989.

Surette, John. Founder of the Spiritearth centre and network, now based at The Well, an eco-spirituality centre in Chicago; see www.csjthewell.org/

Surette, John, 'Epic of evolution: The Jesus connection' from *Spiritearth newsletter,* August 2002, 4–5.

Suzuki, David, with McConnell, Amanda, *The Sacred Balance: rediscovering our place in nature.* Bantam, 1999.

Swimme, Brian, and Thomas Berry, *The Universe Story: a celebration of the unfolding of the Cosmos.* HarperSanFrancisco, 1992.

Swimme, Brian, *Canticle to the Cosmos.* DVD available at www.brianswimme.org

Swimme, Brian, *The Hidden Heart of the Cosmos: Humanity and the New Story.* Maryknoll, NY: Orbis Books, 1996.

Swimme, Brian, *Canticle to the Cosmos.* Study guide to the DVD, edited by Bruce Bochte. New Story Project/Tides Foundation, 1990.

Tacey, David, *The Spirituality Revolution: the emergence of contemporary spirituality.* Brunner-Routledge, 2004.

Taylor, John, *The Go-Between God.* SCM Press, 1972.

Taylor, John, *A Matter of Life and Death,* SCM Press, 1986:3.

Teilhard de Chardin, Pierre, *The Phenomenon of Man.* William Collins, 1955.

Teilhard de Chardin, Pierre, *Hymn of the Universe*. Collins, 1965.

Tolle, Eckhart, *The Power of Now*. Hodder & Stoughton, 2001.

Tomlinson, Dave, *The Post-Evangelical*. London, Triangle, 1995.

Traherne, Thomas, (Dobell's text) *Centuries*. The Faith Press, 1960.

Transition, *The Transition Companion: Making Your Community More Resilient in Uncertain Times*. Transition Books, 2011. See also www.transitionnetwork.org

Uexküll, Jakob von, Opening address of the annual Schumacher lectures in Bristol in 2005 on the theme 'Shaping the Future'.

Underhill, Evelyn, *Mysticism*. Methuen, 1960.

Vanier, Jean, *Community and Growth*. Darton, Longman & Todd, 2nd ed 1989.

Walsch, Neale Donald, *Conversations with God*. Putnam, 1996.

Ward, Hannah, and Jennifer Wild, *Guard the Chaos*. Darton, Longman & Todd, 1995.

Ward, Keith, *A Vision to Pursue: beyond the crisis in Christianity*, SCM Press, 1991.

Watt, Douglas, 'Attachment Mechanisms and the Bridging of Science and Religion' in Clarke, Chris (ed.), *Ways of Knowing: science and mysticism today*. Imprint Academic, Exeter 2005.

White, Lynn, 'The Historical Roots of our Ecological Crisis' first published in *Science*, Vol 155, no. 3767, 10 March 1967, pp. 1203–1207; reprinted in Gottlieb, Roger S. (ed.), *This Sacred Earth: Religion, Nature, Environment*, London: Routledge, 1996.

White, Zoë, *Living Faithfully with Passion*. Birmingham: Woodbrooke, 1992.

White, Zoë, *Preparing the New Age*. Quaker Lesbian and Gay Fellowship, 1993.

Wildwood, Alex, *A Faith to Call Our Own: Quaker tradition in the light of contemporary movements of the Spirit* (Swarthmore Lecture). Quaker Home Service, 1999, reprinted by Quaker Books, 2010.

Wildwood, Alex, *Tradition & Transition: Opening to the sacred yesterday and today*. Pamphlet as issue of *Woodbrooke Journal* No 9, Winter 2001.

Wildwood, Alex; Ashworth, Timothy, and Alex Wildwood, *Rooted in Christianity, Open to New Light: Quaker spiritual diversity.* Pronoun Press/Woodbrooke, 2009.

Williams, Rowan, *Open to Judgement.* Darton, Longman & Todd, 1994.

Windle, Phyllis, 'The Ecology of Grief', in (eds) Roszak, Theodore, Gomes, Mary & Kanner, Allen D. (eds), *Ecopsychology: restoring the Earth, healing the mind.* Sierra Club Books, 1995.

Yungblut, John R., *Shaping a Personal Myth to Live By.* Element Books, 1992.

Lightning Source UK Ltd.
Milton Keynes UK
UKOW04f1211030615

252815UK00001B/16/P